DE PROPRIETATIBUS LITTERARUM

edenda curat

C. H. VAN SCHOONEVELD

Indiana University

Series Maior, 22

INSINUATION
THE TACTICS
OF ENGLISH SATIRE

by

JAMES W. NICHOLS

1971
MOUTON
THE HAGUE · PARIS

LIBRARY OF CONGRESS CATALOG CARD NUMBER: 72-159467

Printed in The Netherlands by Mouton & Co., Printers, The Hague.

To the memory of Porter Perrin

ACKNOWLEDGMENTS

It is a pleasure to be able to record my thanks to Professors Donald S. Taylor and Malcolm Brown of the University of Washington, both of whom read and made helpful comments about an early version of this book; to the Librarian and staff of the former Padelford branch of the University of Washington Library, whose help and frequent indulgence I recall with gratitude; and to the Research and Publication Fund of the University of Southern California for a grant which covered part of the expense of preparing this manuscript for the press. My wife, Ann Eljenholm Nichols, has read each of the several versions of this book and its final argument owes a great deal to her patience, learning, and critical insight.

The dissertation upon which this book ultimately rests began in conversation with Professor Porter Perrin of the University of Washington and was carried to completion under his direction. Whatever virtues this final version may have are in large part owing to his advice and – banal, but necessary word – inspiration.

CONTENTS

I

INTRODUCTION

Everyone evidently agrees what satire is. John Dryden says, "In our modern languages we apply it only to invective poems . . . for in English, to say satire, is to mean reflection, as we use that word in the worst sense; or as the French call it, more properly, *médisance* [*i.e.*, slander]."[1] Dr. Johnson defines a satire as "a poem in which wickedness or folly is censured". According to Evelyn Waugh, "Satire . . . is aimed at inconsistency and hypocrisy. It exposes polite cruelty and folly by exaggerating them. It seeks to produce shame."[2]

All three of these definitions have a common focus – they make it clear that a "satire" is a work in which an unfavorable comment is made, censure is expressed, someone, or something, is blamed. In this they agree with most definitions of satire, nearly all of which emphasize that satire embodies scorn, reproof, some form of verbal attack, though the intensity of the attack ranges from the mildest of chiding to thundering denunciation. Yet, though *Mac Flecknoe, The Vanity of Human Wishes* and *A Handful of Dust* are all "satires" in the sense their authors define the word, they are very different kinds of literary works. They differ in structure, in diction, and even in tone, for the majestic cannonading of *The Vanity of Human Wishes* markedly differs in tone from either of the others.

The problem of finding common denominators in works as apparently disparate as these is, in brief, the problem faced by anyone who tries to account for satire as a genre. If "genre" can be conceived "as a grouping of literary works based, theoretically, upon both outer form (specific meter or structure) and also upon inner form (attitude, tone, purpose – more crudely, subject and audience)" as René Wellek and Austin

---

[1] John Dryden, *The Poetical Works of Dryden*, ed. George R. Noyes, Revised ed. (Cambridge, Massachusetts, 1950), p. 303.
[2] "Fan-Fare", *Life* (April 8, 1946), p. 60.

Warren argue in their influential *Theory of Literature*,[3] the difficulty of treating satire as a genre is patent. While there has been a great deal written about the inner form of "satire", remarkably little has been done to establish the outer one, though there have been, of course, many special studies of individual satirists and the forms they use.

"Form" may be the wrong word, for most modern critics would agree with Robert Elliott that satire "has lost for us any sense of formal specification".[4] However, there are certain devices, conventions, or – as I have chosen to call them – "tactics", which are highly characteristic of satire. Considered together they suggest, I think, that satire may be a genre in some useful sense of the term. In the pages which follow I have tried to isolate and exemplify what seem to me to be the chief tactics used by British and American satirists – satirists writing IN ENGLISH, as the title of this book is meant to imply. I have not attempted to deal with the drama, though all of the tactics I discuss are to be found there, since the satiric effect of a play is often profoundly affected by the art of the actor, the director, even the set designer. I have not limited my examples to the towering monadnocks found in most anthologies but have spread my net widely. If my argument is to be of more than passing interest its meshes must hold not only a few leviathans, but also the schools of lesser fry which make up the great bulk of any genre.

[3] 2nd ed. (New York, 1956), p. 221.
[4] *The Power of Satire: Magic, Ritual, Art* (Princeton, 1960), p. 185.

II

A DEFINITION AND SOME DISTINCTIONS

Although satire is universally agreed to be unfavorable criticism of some sort – a verbal attack – some distinctions and a more extended definition are clearly in order. I may begin with the word "attack" itself. Though the word is more frequently coupled with satire than any other, it is hardly satisfactory, since it suggests a violent onslaught too strong to describe the apparently mild raillery of, say, *The Rape of the Lock* or *Nightmare Abbey*. A better word is "aggression", which we use today to cover all sorts of attacks, not only overt armed ones, but economic sanctions, unfriendly propaganda, and internal subversion. Satire too varies in intensity and proceeds to its objective by a variety of means, not all of which are direct and unequivocal.

Not all kinds of aggression are "satire", of course. For example, Wordsworth's sonnet, "The World Is Too Much with Us", is aggressively critical of man's lack of sensitivity to what Nature has to teach him; Billy Graham's sermons are aggressively critical of our failure to heed the words of Christ; an editorial in this morning's newspaper is aggressively critical of the apathy of local voters at the last municipal elections. All are aggressive, yet if all are "satire", so is much of the literature of the past and virtually all of modern literature.

"Satire" is often used in such a sense, of course. Edward Young, in the preface to the satires in *Love of Fame, The Universal Passion*, points out that the word is not "unapplicable to graver compositions. Ethics, Heathen and Christian, and the Scriptures themselves, are, in a great measure, a satire on the weakness and iniquity of men."[1] Similar definitions abound. But a term so generally defined is all but useless as a critical tool. Satire is not merely aggression; it is a certain KIND of aggression. "The World Is Too Much with Us" is not what most of us would call a "satire", though it is aggressive in the sense that it is a mild

---

[1] *The Poetical Works of Edward Young* (London, n.d.), p. 376.

attack upon man's materialism and failure to heed the lessons Nature has to teach him. The following passage taken from Book VII of *The Prelude,* in which Wordsworth describes a preacher he has heard during his residence in London, is aggressive too, but its manner of proceeding is different:

> There have I seen a comely bachelor,
> Fresh from a toilette of two hours, ascend
> His rostrum, with seraphic glance look up,
> And, in a tone elaborately low
> Beginning, lead his voice through many a maze
> A minuet course; and, winding up his mouth,
> From time to time, into an orifice
> Most delicate, a lurking eyelet, small,
> And not only invisible, again
> Open it out, diffusing thence a smile
> Of rapt irradiation, exquisite.[2]

The difference between the aggression in the sonnet and in this passage is that Wordsworth doesn't deliver his criticism of the preacher directly. The aggression is oblique. Instead of telling us what he thinks and feels, he coaxes us to infer it by insinuating that the preacher is a fop whose sermon is too preciously calculated to be deeply felt. Wordsworth might have said roughly what I have said, but part of the peculiar effect of the passage would have evaporated with the direct statement. One part of the effect is dependent upon the indirection as such – it is one thing to be told something directly, but another and often more satisfactory one to be given clues which have to be interpreted. Moreover, and perhaps more important, when we make the effort to respond to the satirist's devices – the ways in which he insinuates – as we must do when we make the effort to understand the passage, we are forced to enter into the satire in a much more intimate way than if we had simply been *told* something – however brilliant the telling itself might be. It is not too much to say that instead of remaining an audience, we become participants in the satire – and hence in a sense satirists ourselves.

"Satire", then, is a certain kind of aggression, oblique or indirect. Though works as different as Defoe's *The True-Born Englishman,* Dryden's *Mac Flecknoe,* and some of the portraits in "The General Prologue" of *The Canterbury Tales* are often lumped together as "satires", doing so obscures very important differences. All are aggres-

[2] *The Poetical Works of Wordsworth,* ed. Thomas Hutchinson (New York, 1933), p. 695.

sive (though with varying degrees of intensity), but the aggression is of different kinds. Each proceeds in a different manner.

There are, I should like to suggest, three main channels in which English satire has flowed from its earliest appearance in English literature. The most distinctive of these channels, the most characteristically "satiric", is the channel of indirect satire.

A second channel of English satire is the channel of direct satire. Alvin Kernan's *The Cankered Muse* discusses this in some detail. Kernan focuses chiefly upon formal verse satire and the satiric drama of Jonson, Marston, and their fellows. He argues that there are three important elements in satire, "Scene", "Satirist", and "Plot". The Scene of the satire, he says, is disorderly, crowded, packed to bursting – it gives the impression of dense, turbulent weight. The Satirist presents himself as a "blunt, honest man with no nonsense about him".[3] Kernan says "the most striking quality of satire is the absence of plot".[4] "The normal 'plot' of satire would appear . . . to be a stasis in which the two opposing forces, the satirist on one hand and the fools on the other, are locked in their respective attitudes without any possibility of either dialectical movement or the simple triumph of good over evil."[5]

Kernan's book is an excellent one in many respects, but like most of us who write about satire he generalizes too broadly upon the basis of the works which particularly interest him. The emphases he describes are not invariable in satire generally, though they are characteristic of one of the channels, direct satire, and particularly its most famous sub-branch, formal verse satire.

Kernan is aware that other kinds of satire exist, of course. He discusses briefly "Menippean" satire, which emphasizes "Scene". In a Menippean satire the satiric effect is the result of the emphases, often subtle ones, of the work as a whole. Works like *Piers Plowman, Volpone* and *The Alchemist* are thus Menippean because the satirist is in the background, rather than the foreground, or he may not appear at all. But the emphasis in Kernan's book is clearly upon the devices used in direct satire, and most of his generalizations are derived from formal verse satire, particularly that written around the turn of the seventeenth century.

Direct satire is characterized by invective, deliberate and direct over-

---

[3] *The Cankered Muse: Satire of the English Renaissance*, Yale Studies in English, CXLII (New Haven and London, 1959), p. 16.
[4] Kernan, *The Cankered Muse*, p. 30.
[5] Kernan, *The Cankered Muse*, p. 31.

statement or hyperbole. Typically the satirist makes a direct, frontal assault upon his target, deliberately overstating his case. The reader does not take what he has to say at face value – nor in most cases is he intended to – but the effect of the deliberate overstatement is to make the reader aware that something is wrong, even though he cannot accept the satirist's statement of the case literally. Direct satire shades into perspectives like invective, flyting, the sermon, and various other forms of direct verbal aggression. Though direct satire, particularly formal verse satire, has traditionally been considered an important part of English satire, its aggressive methods are so close to those of other perspectives that it is best to consider it "satire" in a special, or historical sense. The main channel is indirect satire.

There is a third channel as well. "Mixed" satire is a convenient label for it, since the name suggests the bowl of mixed fruits or *satura* from which our word " satire" is itself derived, and implies the combination of methods drawn from both indirect and direct satire which characterize it. The total effect of mixed satire is the result of a combination of direct and indirect statement, both of which are often used in such close conjunction that it is difficult to separate the ingredients.

These are the main channels. Since each is a channel, rather than a separate stream, there is often a problem in classifying the satires which are close to the line of demarcation. Even when the main characteristics of a satire are clear, admixtures of the other types occur: in Swift's *A Modest Proposal,* clearly an indirect satire, there are some quite direct statements; and often a formal verse satire like Charles Churchill's *The Times* includes touches of inversion or understatement. But the main stream of each channel is clear enough to make the divisions meaningful and critically useful.

Some examples will help to clarify these distinctions. "The General Prologue" to *The Canterbury Tales* is not wholly satiric, but the portraits of the Friar, the Monk, and the Prioress are satiric portraits which well typify the way in which the indirect satirist works. The portrait of the Friar is the more overtly satiric of the three. It begins:

> A Frere ther was, a wantowne and a merye,
> A lymytour, a ful solempne man.
> In alle the ordres foure is noon that kan
> So muchel of daliaunce and fair langage.
> (208-211)[6]

---

[6] Quotations are from *The Poetical Works of Chaucer,* ed. F. N. Robinson (Cambridge, Massachusetts, 1933).

He is "wantowne" and "merye", and knows a good deal about "daliaunce" and "fair langage". The most striking thing about all of the terms is that, in Middle English, they can mean one of two things. Is the Friar merely a jolly cleric, or is he a lascivious one? Or is he both? That he is described as both "merye" and "solempne" emphasizes the ambiguity. The key word is "daliaunce". Playful chatter – or something less innocent? The lines which follow imply an answer:

> He hadde maad ful many a mariage
> Of yonge wommen at his owene cost.
> (211-213)

Nothing has been said directly, but the juxtaposition of "daliaunce" with the information that the friar has married young women at his own expense weights one set of possible meanings. We now suspect that we should interpret them as an implicit commentary on Huberd's lust. The suspicion is confirmed a few lines later when we learn that Huberd is greedy for money. As we read further into the passage we become more sure about how to read it. We can infer that the Friar's words:

> For unto a povre ordre for to yive
> Is signe that a man is wel yshryve;
> For if he yaf, he dorste make avaunt,
> He wiste that a man was repentaunt;
> For many a man so hard is of his herte,
> He may not wepe, althogh hym soore smerte.
> Therfore in stede of wepynge and preyeres
> Men moote yeve silver to the povre freres.
> (225-232)

are to be read as unctuous hypocrisy, since hypocrisy in one thing suggests it in another. We are prepared to draw the proper conclusions from lines like:

> His typet was ay farsed ful of knyves
> And pynnes, for to yeven faire wyves.
> (233-234)

This is a good example of the techniques characteristic of indirect satire. The satirist begins by giving us details which may be interpreted in more than one way. But the further we read, the more aware we become that the details, and the words themselves, have been carefully selected to imply an adverse criticism even though no direct comment may be made.

No norm is mentioned or alluded to within the satiric portrait itself, but Huberd is being measured against the norm brought to the satire by the average reader. How ought a friar to act? However little the reader knows about the clerical orders of the Middle Ages, he must at least know that a good friar must not fornicate or be greedy for money. In other words, whatever a worthy friar does, it is not THAT. If the reader doesn't know the norm, there is no satire as far as he is concerned.

What Chaucer has put into the portrait is important; what he has left out is almost equally so. We are given no details which would extenuate Huberd's conduct. Extenuating details would not utterly destroy the satire, for the typical reader will recognize that no mundane considerations will wholly excuse a friar's neglect of his vows, but they would be likely to weaken the impact.

Friar Huberd's deviation from the conduct expected of a member of a religious order is so sufficiently gross that we needn't be reminded what the norm is. The case of the Monk is somewhat different. The charges against him are less severe, and we may at first be inclined to be lenient with what seem to be small vanities. We are told that he is a "manly man", a lover of horses and the hunt, that he is scornful of labor, fond of finery and good living. We might even manage reluctant admiration for his forthright statement:

> He yaf nat of that text a pulled hen,
> That seith that hunters ben nat hooly men,
> Ne that a monk, whan he is recchelees,
> Is likned til a fissh that is waterlees, –
> This is to seyn, a monk out of his cloystre.
> But thilke text heeld he nat worth an oystre;
> (177-182)

and agree with the narrator's comment "I seyde his opinion was good" (183) were it not that St. Maurus – St. Benedict's disciple – is mentioned in line 173 and St. Augustine's behest to the clergy in lines 184 to 187.

An ideal is being recalled for us, rather than a "norm", but it puts the Monk's words and conduct in another light. He stands condemned by the very standards he himself professes, and which it is clear he is consciously violating. We suddenly realize that the tone of the entire passage is insinuating: that "a fair for the maistrie" (165) is to be taken ironically, that to describe a man of God as "a manly man" is not necessarily unqualified praise, and "to been an abbot able" is not praise of the Monk, but an implicit criticism of the sort of abbot who too frequently presided over medieval monastic orders.

With the character of the Prioress we approach one of the boundaries of satire. It is satiric, I think, but the satire is so light, so gentle, that to say even that Chaucer is being "aggressive" seems an overstatement. Madame Eglentyne is not grossly, sinfully sensual and venal as Huberd is, nor does she seem to consciously and deliberately violate the spirit of her order, as the Monk does his.

No one detail, but rather an accumulation of them, produces the satiric effect. The fact that some of the words used to describe her are from the stock vocabulary of the romantic poets, the detailed description of her perhaps over-nice manners at table, the conscious dignity and courtliness of her bearing, the fact that the motto her brooch bears – *Amor vincit omnia*[7] – is at least as applicable to the mundane as to the spiritual world – all these suggest that there is just a shade too much of the world, a touch too little of the cloister, in her make-up.

The details Chaucer gives us are important; those absent are worthy of mention, too. Where are the qualities of self-abnegation, holiness and devotion to God which we might expect in a Prioress? We see only a few outward signs; there is nothing in her portrait which suggests the inner spiritual qualities of the Parson. Even the tender feelings, the charity and the compassion which are mentioned are excited by the sight of a mouse caught in a trap.

I have mentioned two sorts of context already – that which the reader brings to the satire, and that which is implied by references within the satiric portrait, like the references to the Prioress' rosary and brooch. A third sort of context is also important. This is the context provided by the Prologue as a whole. Neither the Monk nor the Prioress is pilloried, but both are implicitly criticized for being too much of one world, too little of another. The other world by whose standards they fall short is the world which they themselves have chosen, namely, the world of the spirit. The existence of this world is constantly brought to our attention in *The Canterbury Tales,* not only by idealized portraits like that of the Parson, nor by references to saints and martyrs or incidental details, but by the very fact that *The Canterbury Tales* is the record of what

---

[7] *Amor vincit omnia*: the words from Virgil's Tenth Eclogue set the seal on Chaucer's portrait of the Prioress. The words are those of Gallus, who has lost the woman he loves and tries to forget his suffering by devoting himself to pastoral pursuits. But to no avail. Love can never be forgotten; it carries all before it. The words from a pagan poem about sensual love had been given a Christian meaning – Christ's love overcomes all things, too. But the fact that the Prioress has chosen to wear them reveals in a flash the mixture of qualities with which she is endowed – the self-conscious woman who is imperfectly concealed in the ecclesiastical habit.

happens on a pilgrimage to the tomb of the "hooly blisful martir", St. Thomas Becket at Canterbury.[8]

Daniel Defoe's *The True-Born Englishman* is a typical direct satire. It was written in 1701, when William of Nassau was under attack although the benefits of the Glorious Revolution he had led were assured. William's dour personality and his unpopular foreign policy were the chief causes of discontent, but much of the popular outcry was directed against the fact that he was a foreigner, a Dutchman, and that many of his supporters, who had been rewarded for their services to him and to England, were foreign-born.

Defoe's target is English false pride and ingratitude – ingratitude to William and his foreign supporters who had served the nation well, and the false pride of the English who prided themselves upon the purity of the English "race". Defoe assumes the stock role of the Satirist. The Satirist's characteristics are implicit in the poem itself, but in "An Explanatory Preface" which was added to the ninth of the many editions of the poem, they are made explicit as well. The situation, the Satirist says, "is so plain, that he who is ignorant of it, is too dull to be talk'd with" (p. 25).[9] "If I have fallen rudely upon our Vices, I hope none but the Vicious will be angry. As for Writing for Interest I disown it; I have neither *Place* nor *Pension,* nor *Prospect:* nor *seek none,* nor will *have none:* If matter of Fact justifies the Truth of the Crimes, the *Satyr* is just" (27). He apologises for the "hasty Errors" of the verse, but says that he has "all Along strove rather to make the Thoughts Explicite, than the Poem Correct" (27-28).

The role Defoe assumes here is an eighteenth-century version of the Satirist of the Renaissance formal verse satire and of direct satire generally – an honest, plain-spoken man speaking disinterestedly against vice, a man who is too interested in truth to pay attention to mere "correctness". I use "Satirist" to describe the speaker of the poem because it is important to recognize that the "I" of direct satire is a conventional part taken by the writer of the satire. There is no reason to doubt that Defoe is perfectly sincere in his espousal of the cause of William and his Dutch supporters; all the evidence we have confirms this. But the way in which this support is manifested is not to have

---

[8]   A good discussion of these aspects of *The Canterbury Tales* is Arthur W. Hoffman, "Chaucer's Prologue to Pilgrimage: The Two Voices", *ELH, A Journal of English Literary History*, XXI (1954), 1-16.
[9]   Quotations are from *The Novels and Selected Writings of Daniel Defoe*, Vol. XIV (Oxford, 1927).

Defoe speak AS Daniel Defoe, but to utilize a stock figure who will do the speaking for him.

The Satirist begins by describing the racial strains of Europe and their prevailing vices – the Pride of Spain, the Lust of Italy, the Drunkenness of Germany. England shares the vices of all the races which have contributed to her blood line, it becomes apparent, but is possessed particularly by one of her own:

> *Ingratitude*, a Devil of *Black Renown*,
> Possess'd her very early for his own.
> An Ugly, Surly, Sullen, Selfish Spirit,
> *Who* Satan's *worst Perfections does Inherit*
> (36)

He describes the peoples who have come to England, the Romans, Gauls, Greeks, Lombards, and all the conquering hordes until the time of William the Conqueror, and says:

> All these their Barb'rous Off-spring left behind
> The Dregs of Armies, they of all Mankind; . . . .
>
> From this Amphibious Ill-born Mob began
> *That vain ill natur'd thing, an* Englishman.
> (37)

And, lest his readers argue that time has softened imported vices:

> And lest by Length of Time it be pretended,
> The Climate may this Modern Breed ha' mended;
> Wise Providence to keep us where we are,
> Mixes us daily with exceeding Care:
> We have been *Europes's* Sink, the *Jakes* where she
> Voids all her Offal Out-cast Progeny.
> (39)

This is perfectly direct. There is no difficulty about recognizing the point the Satirist is making. But the reader also recognizes that the Satirist is grossly overstating his case.

Overstatement is the essential characteristic of direct satire. The audience may not, in most cases probably does not, accept what the Satirist says at face value, but recognizes that there is some merit in the Satirist's case and responds with pleasure to his vigorous statement of it. The delighted cries "Give 'em Hell, Harry!" which regularly punctuated the speeches of that fine direct Satirist Harry Truman in 1948 are typical responses to good direct satire. President Truman's audiences were well aware that he was overstating the case against the

Republicans, but delighted in suspending an everyday necessity to be "fair" and responding fully to the virtuosity of his attack. This pure enjoyment of exaggeration which plays a part in the reader's response to direct satire is thus doubtless enjoyment of the grotesque for its own sake. The figure of the Satirist plays a part too. Although he is first of all a device for dramatising and describing the overblown scene of the direct satire, the grotesqueness of his personality, whether it is described for the reader explicitly or merely implied, contributes to the effect.

Though overstatement is the hallmark of the direct satire, as I have said, there may be touches of inversion or understatement; the gross overstatement may subside to something which seems to be fairly close to a reasonable representation of the facts as they would appear to an unbiased outsider. Like other direct satires, particularly long ones, the technique of *The True-Born Englishman* varies. But the essential marks of its channel are plainly evident.

If indirect satire, primarily oblique aggression, and direct satire, mainly direct aggressive overstatement, represent two clearly defined channels, there is obviously an intermediate area as well, an area into which a good many satires fall. Their manner of proceeding is partly direct, partly indirect, and "mixed" satire is a convenient way of labelling them. Dryden's *Mac Flecknoe* is a familiar example. The poem has strong elements of direct overstatement; Flecknoe, the old monarch, says:

> Sh–alone my perfect image bears,
> Mature in dulness from his tender years:
> Sh–alone, of all my sons, is he
> Who stands confirm'd in full stupidity.[10]
> (15-18)

But other devices are used in conjunction with overstatement. The rhythm of the lines, particularly the opening lines, is stately – heroic and solemnly philosophical. This very movement helps achieve an effect of mock grandeur which is central to the effect of the poem. Moreover, we are not merely told Mac Flecknoe is dull; his dulness is dramatized for us. We are present at a mock coronation, described in detail – wittily ludicrous detail. The details of Mac Flecknoe's physical appearance, his speech from the coronation throne, the eulogy of the retiring monarch – all help to realize Mac Flecknoe. He becomes dulness incarnate. In other poems which we rather loosely lump together as

---

[10] *The Poetical Works of Dryden,* ed. George R. Noyes (Cambridge, Massachusetts, 1950), p. 134.

"mock-heroic", similar combinations of aggressive tactics are used. *The Dunciad* contains passages of direct overstatement, but the dunces are not merely called dunces, their qualities are dramatized for us. In *Absalom and Achitophel* the narrator speaks out directly often enough, but what he has to say is conveyed indirectly as well. There are implicit parallels between the Biblical David and King Charles, and between David's son Absalom and the Duke of Monmouth. The temptation of Absalom by Achitophel has its parallels in the temptation of Eve by Satan, and of Christ by Satan. Parallels like this insinuate a meaning which is not stated directly.

In some other mixed satires the combination of tactics is largely verbal. Poems like Swift's "Verses on the Death of Dr. Swift", and Pope's *Moral Essays* and *Imitations of Horace* frequently shift from direct statement to irony. Shifts like these complicate the reading of a mixed satire, since the "set" with which the reader begins must be continually adjusted. Constant shifting of set is characteristic of satire in general, but it is particularly marked in mixed satire. But, though "mixed" is a convenient category, we need not examine examples in detail here, for the most interesting devices of mixed satire are the same as those of indirect satire itself. The most fruitful way of looking at mixed satire is, I think, to consider it a variety of indirect satire in which direct overstatement is used to contrast with and intensify the effect of the aggressive devices used in indirect satire.

Satire, then – to continue the definition – is not only aggression, it is in its most characteristic form oblique or indirect aggression, and the channels I have called "direct" and "mixed" satire above, though related, are less central. Aggression against whom? The objects of satire, at least as satirists and many of their critics profess to see them, are neatly summed up by Samuel Johnson and Evelyn Waugh, both of whom I quoted earlier. Johnson argues that a satire censures "wickedness and folly", Waugh that it exposes "cruelty" as well.[11] These are perfectly traditional statements and, in a perfectly traditional way, beg the basic question of what constitutes "wickedness", "folly", and "cruelty". The answer of course is obvious – the satirist himself determines this and, if

---

[11]   Both Johnson and Waugh are satirists themselves and thus, one might argue, not wholly disinterested critics. However, their statements can be paralleled in many discussions of satire by non-satirists – *e.g.* Gilbert Highet, in *The Anatomy of Satire* (Princeton, New Jersey, 1962): "The purpose of satire is, through laughter and invective, to cure folly and to punish evil; but if it does not achieve this purpose, it is content to jeer at folly and to expose evil to bitter contempt." (p. 156).

he is successful, persuades us that his vision is in some sense a true one. But folly, like beauty, exists in the eye of the beholder, and a much more accurate way of describing a satire from the audience's point of view is to say it is a work in which the author moves aggressively against what is MADE TO SEEM worthy of blame.

The emphasis given "made to seem" is worth dwelling upon for a moment, since the fact that the satirist manipulates our response to achieve the satiric effect is basic to the thesis of this book. A little later I shall argue that the art of the satirist consists largely of employing devices to manipulate point of view. Let me anticipate the argument here. To most readers of *Mac Flecknoe,* Thomas Shadwell has become synonymous with dulness. Yet Aubrey counted him "the best comedian we have now" [12] and some critics of Restoration comedy would include him among the best English comic dramatists.[13] A number of contemporary critics ranked Ambrose Philips' pastoral poems above those by Alexander Pope,[14] yet the readers of Pope's *Guardian* Essay Number 40 are unlikely to take Philips as seriously as he may deserve to be taken.

The real merits of Shadwell and Philips, of course, are not an issue here. What is an issue is that the treatment of Shadwell and of Philips' pastorals is a relative one, and that the opinion most readers have of Shadwell and Philips is the result of artistic manipulation of the "facts" of the case, whatever they may be.

We have some information upon which to base an alternative opinion of Shadwell and Philips. We have no corresponding information upon which to base an independent opinion of Wordsworth's preacher, or of the Friar, the Monk, or the Prioress. Yet the same general impression emerges from these portraits. We are not reading impartial accounts; the satirist has "loaded" the portrait to create a blameworthy impression. Another set of details, other emphases – in short, another point of view – would have created quite a different impression. The satirist then is creative in this sense: he not only singles out targets, he selects, shapes and defines. In a very real sense the fops and fools, the dunces and the knaves were not fops, fools, dunces and knaves before he made us recognize them as such. The satirist creates the object of his satire

[12]   Quoted in "Introduction" to *The Squire of Alsatia,* in *Plays of the Restoration and Eighteenth Century,* ed. Dougald MacMillan and Howard Mumford Jones (New York, 1931), p. 257.
[13]   James Sutherland, *English Satire* (Cambridge, 1958), p. 54.
[14]   See George Sherburn, *The Early Career of Alexander Pope* (Oxford, 1934), p. 116.

in much the same way that the artist in any genre shapes the material he has abstracted from life.

Satire is directed against what is made to seem blameworthy. The phrase suggests another consideration. If something is "made to seem blameworthy", there evidently must be some base point from which blame can be measured. We can scarcely have blame in a vacuum. Two generalizations are frequently made about satiric norms, but neither seems to be widely applicable enough to be useful. Some satirists and some critics have argued that the satirist bases aggression upon the conservative values of his time. But if the satirist were merely conservative, he would not be looked upon with such grave suspicion. Byron, Swift and Burns frequently attack the "conservative" values of their times. All satire, insofar as it is aggressive, tends to be upsetting. An attack upon a part, even a corrupt part, of the whole is likely to be in effect an attack upon the whole. In at least this sense, then, the satirist is hardly conservative; he is in fact a sort of revolutionary.[15]

Sometimes another kind of general norm is suggested. The satirist is likely to say, or strongly imply, that he measures human conduct or the results of human conduct, by a norm with which all reasonable men will agree. However, since he is at least ostensibly attacking "abuses" of reason, it is natural for him to adopt the attitude that he is DEFENDING reason and that all sensible men will agree with him. Two satirists may of course take opposite points of view on the same issue, as frequently happened in the eighteenth century. On a given measure Robert Walpole might be attacked by a group of satirists, while the opponents of the measure were in turn attacked by a group of Walpole's minion satirists, both arguing that they were defending "reason". It is hardly profitable to argue that satire defends reason if by the word we mean a fixed and invariable standard which can be accepted as the norm of more than one satirist, of more than one work by the same satirist, or even within the same work by the same satirist, for satirists frequently shift their ground. In fact the satirist's profession that he is on the side of reason is itself one of his satiric techniques.

Satiric norms pose further difficulties. One reason it is difficult to discuss them is that they often resist formulation in precise terms. By what norms are Wordsworth's preacher, Chaucer's Friar and Monk being evaluated? We aren't told directly. In the case of the preacher and the Friar it is hard to formulate precise, positive norms, since we

[15] See Robert C. Elliott, "The Satirist and Society", *ELH, A Journal of English Literary History*, XXI (1954), 248.

are shown not how they should, but how they SHOULD NOT act. The case of the Monk is a little different, for St. Maurus and St. Augustine are mentioned and this very fact insinuates a norm.[16] But the narrator of "The General Prologue" doesn't tell us this – we must infer it. It is perfectly true, of course, that most readers of all three satiric passages will bring some ideas about right conduct to the satire, but equally true is that no two of these readers will agree precisely what the norm is, where the lines should be drawn.

The norms by which we should judge the Prioress are even more difficult to establish. Some readers have argued that her portrait is not satiric at all – in effect that Chaucer has not clearly established a norm from which she deviates. Obviously the problem of norms is a basic one in satire. The satirist must establish a norm without stating it directly. Since it is unstated, readers' opinions about its boundaries are sure to differ. If the satirist makes deviations from an implied norm gross and unmistakable, the satire is likely to be crude. If the deviation is relatively slight, the satire may be subtler, but the satirist runs the risk of being misunderstood.

Probably most readers of the portraits of the preacher, the Friar, and the Monk, at least, could accept Wordsworth's and Chaucer's norms not only within the context of the satire but outside it as well. The norms, in other words, are based upon general attitudes which most readers share. A different kind of problem arises in satires where the norms the satirist wants his readers to accept are so personal and so idiosyncratic that they can hardly be said to correspond with any generally accepted system of values – or even to be a "system" at all. Most of Thomas Love Peacock's novels are unquestionably satires, yet the norms Peacock uses are exceedingly difficult to state in general terms, and all but defy rational analysis.[17] Samuel Butler says in *Hudibras*, "Men fell out, they knew not why". Since he leaves the explicit reasons for the actions of the characters in the poem at that, we must

---

[16] "Ideal" is a better word than "norm" in cases like this, since the standard is higher than normal human behavior, but I shall use "norm" throughout for simplicity's sake.

[17] As Ronald Mason says in his fine appreciation of Peacock, "At times he seems to be using his admirable clarity of expression, his forthright inimitable critical prose, to gratify a splenetic whim engendered by over-indulgence. He hits, and hits hard, not for the reason that the object of his attack has offended against any canon of taste or morals, but because it has happened in the eccentricity of his own mood to annoy him personally." ("Notes for an Estimate of Peacock", in *The Golden Horizon*, ed. with an introduction by Cyril Connolly [London, 1953], p. 525.)

assume that his characters are being satirized for their lack of good sense. What defines "good sense"? Obviously, the satirist himself. The norm of the poem is really Butler's own sense of fitness[18] and what this sense of fitness is, is made clear only in the poem itself and not simply by measuring the characters and events of the poem by an external scale of values.

I have suggested that the norms of satire need not be based upon a received body of opinion, nor based upon "reason", nor stated or implied with great precision, nor even be consistent or congruent with norms the reader would accept outside the context of the satire. Though the satiric norm may be more effective if it conforms to norms acceptable outside the context of the satire, it does not depend upon them for much the same reason that a poet's success does not absolutely depend upon the truth or consistency of his philosophy. If the poet is a good poet, a poem may be artistically convincing whether or not it is philosophically acceptable. Similarly, a satire may be effective whether or not the reader would accept its norms outside the satire. The whole matter may be summed rather briefly. A satiric norm is essentially a vantage point from which something else may be viewed. Since it is a means to an end, rather than an end in itself, it may work successfully if the satiric view is a satisfying one. What use the satirist makes of it, what happens within the satire, is crucial.

The norms necessary to satire are frequently created, or enforced, within the satire itself. But these norms have an obvious relationship to the norms brought by the reader to the satire, norms which are largely set by the reader's total experience of the world. These are created by factors too complex to be more than sketched here, but they include the reader's store of factual and historical knowledge, his religious and moral training, his experience of life, his reading, his temperament – in short the combined cultural and personal influences which determine how he looks at the world and what he thinks "right" or at least "fitting and proper". This whole complex of ideas and emotions is the context in which a satire exists. One way of defining satire would be to say that it is the systematic exploitation, with aggressive intent, of what are, or are made to seem, deviations from the norm within a context.

The context brought to a satire varies from reader to reader. Even

---

[18] Butler's "norm" is discussed in Edward Ames Richards, *Hudibras in the Burlesque Tradition*, Columbia University Studies in English and Comparative Literature, CXXVII (New York, 1937), p. 131; and Dan Gibson, Jr., "Samuel Butler", *Seventeenth Century Studies*, ed. Robert Shafer (Princeton, 1933), p. 283.

contemporaries may differ about whether a given work is a "satire" or not because each brings a different context to it. Time lapses and changing cultural conditions affect a context as well. To a modern audience, some of the projects Swift satirizes in Part III of *Gulliver's Travels* seem scarcely as absurd as he and his original audience presumably thought them. Changing political conditions have reduced or destroyed the satiric effect of some of Defoe's pamphlets, and only a resolute scholar can fully appreciate the social, literary, political and musical satire in *The Beggar's Opera*. The point of the satire on the Italian operas current in Gay's day, and on the political conditions of the time, has been largely lost.

In the case of *The Beggar's Opera* the change in the reader's context is largely the result of the loss of certain kinds of historical knowledge. Failure to bring a certain kind of knowledge to a satire may affect even a contemporary reader's response to a satire, also. This frequently happens when someone outside the inner circle reads a coterie satire and is puzzled. He may be aware of the presence of certain satiric DEVICES, yet not know precisely what the object of the satire is, or how he is expected to respond. Doubtless some satires have "vanished" altogether because no one is able to bring to them the proper context – and some intended satire (satire which does not "come off") is not distinguishable as satire because the author has miscalculated the context which his readers will bring to it.

Changing conditions may work the other way, too; they may make a work which originally was not intended or read as a satire seem satiric. Some romantic poetry – Coleridge's "To a Young Ass" for example – seems satiric to a modern audience, and there are many passages in *The Man of Feeling* which have, to a twentieth-century reader, a satiric flavor not intended by the author and not taken as satire by his contemporaries.

Although one may speak of a "satiric" view of life, as one may of a "comic," or "tragic" one, critics of satire are seldom willing to leave it at this. Though from one point of view the satirist is a creator and shaper of material he has drawn from experience and thus is simply another kind of literary artist, the personality of the writer of the satire intrudes into criticism in ways that are less common in discussion of other literary forms. Satire is often personal, sometimes seems malicious, and thus frequently appears so bound up with the personality of its creator that it is natural to speculate about the motives which impel him.

Sometimes, for reasons that are easy enough to understand, the inquiry is misdirected, for the reader of satire may mistake some of the characters created by the satirist for the satirist himself. The Elizabethan formal verse satirists, basing their ideas upon a misreading of classical theory and practice, associated the satirist with the "satyr". They saw him as a rude railer, a rough country dweller come to town to deliver a philippic against his city cousins. Elizabethan writers of satire assumed the role of the satyr and were frequently identified with their dramatic creations. Even modern critics sometimes make this assumption. John Peter, in *Complaint and Satire in Early English Literature,* argues that John Marston himself was a frenzied, incoherent schizophrenic because the speaker of his satires seems to be one.[19] The writers of other kinds of satire, too, are sometimes identified in a quite literal way with the characters of their works, or some of the views expressed in them. Swift's and Pope's are the most familiar cases. Swift has often been called a savage misanthrope because Gulliver becomes one. Pope was portrayed in Lytton Strachey's memorable essay as a fiendish little dwarf gleefully ladling boiling oil on the heads of his enemies.

A good deal of recent scholarship on satire has been devoted to establishing one point which I shall touch upon briefly here and return to later. The point is simply that a speaker, or character in a satire, whether he be an unnamed narrator, a persona, a fictional character, even – as he is in some cases – a speaker who is literally identified as the writer of the satire, is first and foremost an artistic creation shaped to serve the purposes of the satire. What is crucial, in other words, is not his possible biographical significance, but his rhetorical function. It is obviously misleading to assume that the views of a fictional creation must be identical with those of his creator even in direct satire; the error is compounded in satire, where the very essence of the manner of proceeding is to convey a meaning by indirection.

But even if the satirist is not identified literally with his characters, other charges remain at his door. He appears to exhibit an unnatural preoccupation with discreditable subjects. He is suspected of an unhealthy interest in abnormality. He frequently deals with identifiable persons and specific historical events. Since the satiric view of these is aggressive, the satirist is stigmatized as malicious. These are serious charges and any critic of satire, whether or not he chooses to "defend" the satirist, or to try to give satire in general a better "character", must deal with them. Three points seem to be worth at least brief discussion.

---

[19]   (Oxford, 1956), pp. 174-175.

First, the satirist typically defends himself and his work by arguing that satire is intended to chastise the foolish or vicious, and to reform them. I have already suggested that it is the satirist himself who determines what is foolish or vicious, and while we cannot generalize about the justness of the satirist's aggression, we can agree that satire is often a very effective instrument of punishment. It is true that the objects of some forms of satiric aggression appear to have shrugged off the satire (we recall Sir Robert Walpole leading the applause at the first performance of *The Beggar's Opera,* and Lord Chesterfield proudly showing Johnson's famous letter to his friends and visitors), but there is a good deal of evidence, too, that prospective targets walked lightly in the presence of Pope and Charles Churchill, and it is incontestable that a number of reputations have suffered all but irreparable damage as a result of satiric attacks. We need only recall the damage to their reputations suffered by Cibber, Shadwell, Ambrose Philips, the great Duke of Marlborough, whose character Swift continued to attack even after his death, to be convinced that the satirist may punish very effectively, whether or not he is able to "reform" the objects of his aggression in any observable way.

"Reformation", of course, is another matter. Most satirists have at least professed to be impelled to write satire by a desire to bring the object of the aggression to the bar of penitence. Defoe, for example, says "The end of Satyr is reformation: and the Author, tho' he doubts the Work of Conversion is at a general Stop has put his Hand to the Plow."[20] Most readers are wary of accepting statements like this at face value, for Defoe, like most satirists who have discussed their art, is defending satire from its detractors. The reason for the somewhat wearisome emphasis upon reformation, we might infer, is an attempt to bring satire into the more respectable company of other forms of literature. Literature, generations of critics have averred (taking a defensive stance themselves), is for delight and instruction. But to concede that the satirist *delights* in flaying the object of the satire, in causing pain, in blackening reputations, or, incidentally, that his audience takes pleasure in these things, seems discreditable. The emphasis therefore has to fall upon the second half of the definition. Satire must be a kind of instruction. The satirist must be a moralist whose function is to pillory the foolish and vicious with the grand object of making them reform.

The argument has never been a wholly convincing one. For one

---

[20] "Preface" to *The True-Born Englishman,* in *The Novels and Selected Writings,* XIV, 29.

thing, if the satirist is a would-be reformer, we can hardly conclude that he has been markedly successful. Fools, like sinners who refuse to attend chapel to be preached at, don't invariably read satire. Even when they do, as Swift observed, they are likely to see other faces than their own in the satirist's mirror.[21] The fact is that the reader of any satire is likely to try to avoid believing that the satire is directed against him, and even in personal satire, where the realization of a Shadwell or Cibber is inescapable, he is sure to protest "But that's not the *real* me!" And of course he is often right. The satirist manipulates the "facts" of the case. If we accept the satirist's argument that he is attempting to reform individuals we must also recognize that he is fatuously optimistic and hence rather foolish himself.

We needn't – to bring up a second point – take "reformation" quite so narrowly of course. Even if the object of a satire is unwilling, or incapable of, amending the vices and follies for which he has originally been satirized, he may be afraid of further ridicule and hence more circumspect, and those who see in a satire vices, follies, foibles of which they themselves are guilty, may be moved to future amendment. Doubtless also some satiric works have been effective instruments of social reform and progress. (*The Drapier's Letters* had a decisive effect upon Irish public opinion.) Some satiric novels – we think of some of Dickens' novels, and a number of other, even more frankly, vehicles of propaganda – have had a measurable effect upon public opinion and have contributed to movements for reform. However, the difficulty with citing examples like these is that while many of them may be included under a very general heading labelled "satire", they seem to be near its fringes. Moreover, most of the works I might cite seem to be direct satires, or if they are satires in the sense I have defined it, are ones in which the indirection is minimal. Most of us would agree that though satire may serve as an instrument of propaganda and lead to reform, these effects are by-products. We must look elsewhere for the essential aims and effects of satire.

If satire is ineffective as an agent of moral suasion, and is only incidentally an incentive to general reform, it might be argued that while the sensitive and serious reader of satire may not be able or willing to amend the abuses the satirist points out, through satire he may arrive at a greater knowledge both of himself and of mankind in general. Thus the reader is inclined in the direction of right action in the future even though he may not do anything about present abuses. This is possible,

[21]   "The Preface of the Author" to *The Battle of the Books*.

of course, and is one way of "justifying" satire to its opponents. But this explanation hardly accounts for the particular effect of satire, for greater awareness of self and the world in general is one of the aims of all literature. We must come to a third point, or come back, really, for it was the springboard for the present discussion. The point is that satire is, in a sense, malicious – or, to put it in another way, aggression is a source of pleasure to the satirist, and to his audience as well. This is not to say that some satirists in some of their works may not be actuated by a genuine desire to reform the objects of their satire, that they may not hope, at least, that some good will come of their work. But, quite clearly, not all satirists are actuated by these motives, and if we want to arrive at some general statement which seems to apply to all satire we shall have to merely note these possibilities in passing. We cannot assume that all satirists are moved by altruism. What we may say with some assurance is, not that all satirists aim to reform and amend, but that PROFESSIONS of intent to reform and amend are common satiric tactics. The devices of satire, like those of rhetoric, may be employed with all sorts of motives.

In an essay which first appeared in the Irish *Intelligencer,* Jonathan Swift said:

There are two Ends that Men propose in writing Satyr; one of them less noble than the other, as regarding nothing further than the private Satisfaction, and Pleasure of the Writer; but without any View towards *personal Malice:* The other is a *publick Spirit,* prompting Men of *Genius* and Virtue, to mend the World as far as they are able. And as both these Ends are innocent, so the latter is highly commendable. With regard to the former, I demand, whether I have not as good a Title to laugh, as Men have to be ridiculous; and to expose Vice, as another hath to be vicious. If I ridicule the Follies and Corruptions of a *Court,* a *Ministry,* or a *Senate,* are they not amply paid by *Pensions, Titles,* and *Power;* while I expect, and desire no other Reward, than that of laughing with a few Friends in a Corner?[22]

Swift's arguments that a Public Spirit prompts the satirist to attempt to mend the world, and that the satirist is not actuated by personal malice need no comment. They are variations of the justifications of satire we have already considered. But the frank statement that one of the ends of writing satire is "the private Satisfaction, and Pleasure of the Writer" and of his friends is a less common admission, for satirists are often unwilling to admit that pleasure is one of their chief motives. It

[22] *The Prose Works of Jonathan Swift,* ed. Herbert Davis (Oxford, 1939-1962), XII (1955), 34.

seems discreditable to admit that one enjoys satisfying aggressive impulses. Yet there is no doubt that most of us enjoy reading or listening to satire, enjoy participating in the flaying of those who are made to seem fools and knaves, and it seems reasonable to assume that our pleasure has its counterpart in the pleasure the satirist takes in initiating the aggression.

Swift is content to state, rather than develop, his point, but Sigmund Freud in *Jokes and Their Relation to the Unconscious*, his chief contribution to aesthetics, has a number of things to say which seem to suggest reasons why the satirist enjoys writing satire and we enjoy reading it. Freud argues that the maker of a joke draws upon two sources of pleasure. First, there is the pleasure inherent in the manipulation of language or of idea which is the basis of the joke. The pleasure depends upon the technique because both pleasure and joke itself disappear if the "meaning" of the joke is stated in a non-joking way. A second and very important kind of pleasure arises when the joke "will allow us to exploit something ridiculous in our enemy which we could not, on account of obstacles in the way, bring forward openly or consciously; . . . the joke *will evade restrictions and open sources of pleasure that have become inaccessible.*" [23] He places great stress upon the pleasure which comes from evading restrictions, either internal or external.[24] Internal restrictions are those which inhibit making the joke in the first place. The most far-reaching of these are various kinds of internal "repressions", including an aesthetic objection to speaking or writing overt invective.[25] The external restrictions are those which exist because authority makes it dangerous to express hostility or aggressiveness, or because society frowns upon expressing hostile impulses toward our fellowmen.[26] These pleasures are often the result of attacks upon individuals, but are by no means restricted to them. The same pleasures are available, Freud makes clear, in aggressions against "institutions, people in their capacity as vehicles of institutions, dogmas of morality or religion, views of life which enjoy so much respect that objections to them can only be made under the mask of a joke and indeed of a joke concealed by its façade".[27]

Although Freud's whole discussion of jokes is of the greatest interest

[23]   Trans. and ed. James Strachey (New York, 1963), p. 103. The italics are in the original.
[24]   Freud, *Jokes*, pp. 102 ff.
[25]   See Freud, *Jokes*, pp. 104 and 134, particularly.
[26]   Freud, *Jokes*, pp. 102-103 and *passim*.
[27]   Freud, *Jokes*, pp. 108-109.

to the student of satire, I won't attempt to summarize the complex psychological factors which, Freud argues, enable jokes to produce the kind and quantity of pleasure they do. It will be sufficient for our present purposes merely to indicate what seem to be the most suggestive inferences which we can draw from Freud's study. A good deal of what he has to say applies to all kinds of satire, for even in direct satire we can assume the satirist derives pleasure from satisfying aggressive impulses, and additional pleasure from the devices he uses to mount the satiric aggression – from handling the tools of his trade. What Freud has to say is particularly relevant to indirect satire, for the manner of proceeding in indirect satire and the satisfaction which results from the satiric aggression seem markedly similar to the techniques which are involved in joke-making and the pleasure derived from making a joke. We can go further. Freud says that some kinds of "tendentious jokes" (that is, jokes with a purpose, an object beyond mere innocent fun) serve the purpose of "aggressiveness, satire, or defense . . .".[28] Obviously, this kind of joke *is* a brief satire.

Two sources of pleasure, then, seem to be available to the indirect satirist. One of these is the pleasure inherent in the manipulation of the satiric techniques themselves. As Dryden says, "How easy it is to call rogue and villain, and that wittily! But how hard to make a man appear a fool, a blockhead, or a knave, without using any of these opprobrious terms! . . . This is the mystery of that noble trade . . ."[29] Doubtless this satisfaction has its parallel in the aesthetic satisfaction any artist takes in the creation of the thing he has made. However, the second source of pleasure seems to be peculiar to indirect satire. This is the pleasure which results from the overcoming of restrictions which hinder the expression of aggressive impulses. The indirection itself, in other words, enables the satirist to tap sources of pleasure which are denied to other writers, even writers of direct satire. It seems clear that any assessment of the reasons the indirect satirist writes must take these pleasures into account.

Freud suggests that the "psychical process provoked by the joke in the hearer is in most cases modelled on that which occurs in its creator".[30] And it seems clear that the pleasure we experience in reading satire seems to be drawn from the same sources as that which moves

---

[28]   Freud, *Jokes*, p. 97.
[29]   *Poetical Works*, p. 313.
[30]   Freud, *Jokes*, p. 134. (Freud makes the point provisionally here, but it is confirmed later.)

the writer of the satire. The techniques the satirist uses produce pleasure for both him and his audience [31] and we share the satirist's pleasure in evading restrictions upon hostile impulses which are placed upon all of us by authority, by society, or by morality. Of the latter, Freud observes "What these jokes [we should read "certain kinds of satires"] whisper may be said aloud: that the wishes and desires of men have a right to make themselves acceptable alongside of exacting and ruthless morality." [32] These wishes and desires are natural and legitimate and one of the functions of satire is to allow us to respond to them in a way that would be impossible in the world outside the sphere of the satire where there are all sorts of obstacles to a full unleashing. They may be thwarted not only by authority, by social pressures, by morality, but also by an uneasy conscience which tells us that there are few human beings who are entirely foolish or villainous and few human situations in which right or wrong lie entirely on one side. The satirist's world is one in which the standards he adopts are made to seem the "right" ones. Often the satirist's world is one in which black and white predominate. The son of Flecknoe is not just dull, he is Dulness incarnate. The oppressors of the lower-class Irish are not merely mildly oppressive, but heartless fiends who might seriously consider a proposal to dine on the flesh of children. The inhabitants of Aldous Huxley's *Brave New World* have lost all contact with the human condition. Even in milder satires, the satirist usually gives the opposition no quarter; as a result his readers can allow themselves a satisfying fullness of emotional response which they seldom feel in the real world without all sorts of qualifications and inhibitions.

Let me now bring together and re-state the points I have made at some length above. "Satire" is indirect aggression against a target or targets which are made to seem blameworthy within a given context. The motives of the satirist are complex and vary not only from satirist to satirist, but even within the same satire. The satirist may be actuated by a desire to reform, or to correct foolish or vicious sets of ideas or attitudes; however, he is also actuated by the pleasure of employing satiric devices and of evading the usual restrictions put on the expression of aggressive impulses. The effect upon the audience of the satire appears to parallel the impulses which actuate the satirist. The audience may find that the satire makes them aware of certain follies or vices in

[31] Freud, *Jokes*, p. 95.
[32] Freud, *Jokes*, p. 110.

themselves and the world around them and move them to do something. But a good part of the satiric effect depends upon the pleasure produced by the aggression itself, the pleasure of responding to the satirist's devices, and the power these devices have to open sources of pleasure that are normally forbidden in the world outside the one the satirist creates.

If this definition of satire is a convincing one, it may be allowed that a survey of the way in which English satire works, the devices working together which produce the satiric effect, may be a useful one, for there has heretofore been no general study of them. There have been of course some excellent treatments of individual satiric works. There have been studies of individual satirists – particularly of Swift and Pope. And of course there are a number of historical and critical studies of satire generally. But none of these has confined itself to satires in English, and attempted to isolate and discuss the wide range of artifices which produce the unique effect we call the satiric effect.

Before looking into these devices, a word or two about terminology. "Irony" is the word most frequently used to describe the MANNER of proceeding in satire, and I have used it above in a number of places. It is not an entirely satisfactory term, for too many meanings are associated with it. It is sometimes used to refer to an effect rather than manner of proceeding, as in "tragic", "dramatic", or "romantic" irony. Even if we limit the meaning of the word so that it refers only to a manner of proceeding, there are further difficulties. The meaning of irony is often restricted to saying one thing, but meaning its opposite. In other words, irony often means "inversion". Few satires, certainly few of the subtler ones, operate as crudely as this. Often, as we shall see, the manner of proceeding in a satire is to say something which contains only a measure of "truth", and part of the effect of the satire depends upon the reader's sifting out the proportions of "truth" and "falsity". Even if we take irony to mean SAYING one thing, but meaning something which is not necessarily its opposite, we are leaving out an important satiric device – the device of saying NOTHING. Chaucer's portrait of the Prioress fits our definition of satire, but one of the most important of the satiric devices is to leave out certain details. Their very absence implies blame. The juxtaposition of certain kinds of material, though nothing is said about them at all, can be used to imply blame. The best way of describing the manner of proceeding in a satire, I think, is to say that it "insinuates" a meaning. Insinuation suggests both the indirectness and aggressiveness of satire, and covers both verbal and non-verbal implication. Another term is needed to cover specific types of insinuation. A satirist insinuates in a number of ways. The form or pattern in which he chooses to cast his attack is one of these ways. The persona he creates – a dramatic character not to be identified literally with the satirist himself – is another. Each of these may be called a "tactic". A tactic then is one of the artifices used WITHIN a satire (invariably in conjunction with other tactics) to insinuate blame. In the pages which follow I shall use "insinuation" to describe the general way in which the satirist proceeds, and "tactic" to describe the individual devices or artifice.

III

SATIRIC SHOCK

Henri Bergson remarks in his essay *Laughter,* "Our laughter is always the laughter of a group. . . . However spontaneous it seems, laughter always implies a kind of secret freemasonry, or even complicity, with other laughers, real or imaginary."[1] The remark is equally applicable to satire, for in a sense the audience for any satire is a coterie audience, one which has, if only for the moment, certain attitudes in common. Those who see the point belong to the "in" group, those who do not are barbarians, and part of the pleasure we experience in reading or listening to satire is derived from the delicious savor of understanding more, or feeling differently, than the common herd.

The first task of the writer of satire is to establish a vital contact with his audience, to evoke and then to shape its response toward the objects of the satire. In some cases his task is made easier by certain conditions external to the satire itself. His satire may appear in a magazine like *The New Yorker* or a journal like the London *New Statesman* whose audiences are more homogeneous than most, and whose attitudes to certain subjects are already formed in ways which he can exploit. A satirist writing in *The New Yorker* can assume that his audience will share certain attitudes about, say, modern American advertising, or the cultural level of commercial television programs, and can exploit these attitudes with some assurance that he need not forcibly establish or heavily labor his points.

Other satirists whose work is published outside the context provided by the audience of a particular publication may assume that a certain audience is most likely to read their work – an audience whose reactions they can predict. Or the satirist's name and reputation may give him some assurance that those who choose to read or listen to him will expect a certain kind of satiric tone, or at least be prepared to respond to the very slight signals he provides and govern their responses accordingly.

[1] In *Comedy* (Garden City, New York, 1956), p. 64.

It seem likely that Chaucer depended upon a shared, unspoken understanding with the sophisticated, homogeneous audience for which he
wrote and, perhaps, recited *The Canterbury Tales* for many of his satiric
effects. Modern oral satirists like Mike Nichols and Elaine May, or Mort
Sahl, owe a good part of their success to a similar bond between themselves and their audience. The satiric effect of Ronald Firbank's novels,
of Max Beerbohm's *Zuleika Dobson* and of some of Aldous Huxley's
early novels, depends to a large extent upon a community of understanding. Points of view upon which an appreciation of their satire depends
may be largely lost on an outsider.

But not all satirists depend upon exploiting the already formed attitudes of a homogeneous audience. They may wish to rouse and shape
attitudes which are latent, or not exploited easily; they may even wish to
arouse and exploit attitudes which run directly contrary to the ones
their audiences normally hold. The problem these satirists face is two-
fold. First, they must alert their general audience to the fact that they
are writing satire, insinuating a meaning which is not literally stated.
Secondly, they must establish the vital community of attitude, draw the
coterie around them, as it were, if the satire is to be fully effective. The
tactic which is most frequently used to alert the reader, and thus solve the
first part of the problem, is to surprise or shock him. Very frequently this
contributes toward the solution of the second part of the problem as well.

The reader of a satire – I shall say "reader" as a matter of convenience,
although some satires are of course presented orally – begins to read
with a certain kind of expectation or "set" unless he has been warned by
the title, or something outside the satire itself. His set is determined
primarily by the apparent form of the satire – it appears at first glance
to be an essay, an ode, a short story, or any one of the scores of non-
satiric forms into which a satire may be cast. The set will almost invariably be based upon the assumption that the reading should be a normal
or literal one. If this set is not disturbed, the satire is certain to be misread; it may not be recognized as a satire at all. Thus the satirist must
destroy or alter the original set. He usually does this by giving the reader
a jar, by surprising him with some piece of information, some variation
of tone, some discrepancy between what is said and his normal expectation which cannot be accounted for by the original set. I shall call this
surprise satiric "shock", doubtless with some exaggeration of the violence
of the effect in many cases, but the term will serve well enough if we
allow that the intensity of the shock may vary from mild surprise to
considerable astonishment.

Probably the best known and most startlingly effective use of shock is Jonathan Swift's *A Modest Proposal*. Though some readers may conceivably have been put on the alert earlier (by the reference to "A child, *just dropt from its Dam"*, for example, which implies the persona's point of view) for most the projector's bland statement "I have been assured . . . that a young healthy Child, well nursed, is, at a Year old, a most delicious, nourishing, and wholesome Food. . . ."[2] is a bolt from a cloudless sky. Dryden, a great master of establishing tone and adumbrating strategy and tactics in his openings, begins *Mac Flecknoe:*

> All human things are subject to decay,
> And when fate summons, monarchs must obey.
> This Flecknoe found, who, like Augustus, young
> Was call'd to empire, and had govern'd long;
> In prose and verse, was own'd, without dispute,
> Thro' all the realms of *Nonsense*, absolute.

(A seventeenth-century reader probably would have adjusted the set with which he began the poem when "Flecknoe" is mentioned in the third line; "*Nonsense*" in the sixth alerts the modern reader.)[3]

Evelyn Waugh's *The Loved One* opens with a description of a pair of Englishmen sitting in rocking chairs on the veranda of a paint-blistered bungalow. There is a dry water-hole in the foreground; the sound of dry, rustling palm-leaves and "the ever present pulse of music from the neighbouring native huts" is in their ears. They are "the counterparts of numberless fellow-countrymen exiled in the barbarous regions of the world". . .[4]. Only after the barrenness and barbarity of the scene are firmly established does the reader discover that the rude land to which these Englishmen have been exiled is modern Southern California! Nathanael West's *Miss Lonelyhearts* begins:

The Miss Lonelyhearts of the New York *Post-Dispatch* (Are-you-in-trouble? – Do-you-need-advice? – Write-to-Miss Lonelyhearts-and-she-will-help-you) sat at his desk and stared at a piece of white cardboard. On it a prayer had been printed by Shrike, the feature editor.

> *Soul of Miss L, glorify me.*
> *Body of Miss L, nourish me*
> *Blood of Miss L, intoxicate me.*
> *Tears of Miss L, wash me.*

[2]   *Prose Works*, XII (1955), iii.
[3]   The title of the poem, *Mac* (*i.e.,* son of) *Flecknoe* might have alerted the seventeenth-century reader as well, but it is suggestive that Dryden, like many satirists, uses shock anyway to establish the particular kind of satire used in the poem.
[4]   (Harmondsworth, Middlesex, 1951), p. 7.

Oh good Miss L, excuse my plea,
And hide me in your heart,
And defend me from mine enemies.
Help me, Miss L, help me, help me.
In saecula saeculorum. Amen.[5]

The parody of the *Anima Christi* ("Soul of Christ, sanctify me./Body of Christ, save me./Blood of Christ, inebriate me . . ."). shocks the reader and alerts him to the fact that a literal reading of what follows is likely to be an inadequate one. (The reader who knows that the shrike is a bird of prey which sometimes impales its victims on thorns would have gotten a somewhat earlier shock.)

The shock may come early, as it does in the satires I have just mentioned. The shock may be a series of gradually increasing jars, relatively mild at first, but coming to a climax which only the least perceptive reader can miss. Swift's *A Description of a City Shower* is an "imitation" of Virgil's *Georgics*. The reader might have recognized the parody in the first three or four lines, he was likely to in the next eight or ten, and only the dullest contemporary reader could be unaware of Swift's intention by the last three lines:

> Sweepings from Butchers Stalls, Dung, Guts, and Blood,
> Drown'd Puppies, stinking Sprats, all drench'd in Mud,
> Dead Cats and Turnip-Tops come tumbling down the Flood.

which parody the triplet and alexandrine which Swift associates with Dryden and the poets of Charles the Second's reign.[6]

The shock may be entirely delayed until the very end of the satire, where it jolts the reader into the realization that he has been led to accept a situation on terms which are patently inadequate. Shirley Jackson's *The Lottery* is apparently an innocuous story about a small town holiday custom until its shocking last paragraphs reveal the climax of the ritual and force the reader to reconsider the set with which he has been reading the story. The point at which the satirist presumably intends the shock to occur varies from satire to satire. The point at which the reader experiences the shock varies as well, for some readers are naturally more alert or sensitive than others. But whenever the shock does occur, the reader is forced to recognize, and try to account

---

[5] *The Complete Works of Nathanael West* (New York, 1957), pp. 65-66.
[6] See Swift's note to the poem quoted in *The Poems of Jonathan Swift*, ed. Harold Williams, 2nd ed. (Oxford, 1958), I, 139-140; and Maurice Johnson, *The Sin of Wit: Jonathan Swift as a Poet* (Syracuse, 1950), pp. 85-86.

for, something which cannot be fitted into the pre-set pattern of expectation and response which he has brought to the work.

I suspect that most of the original readers of Alexander Pope's *A Key to the Lock* only gradually became aware of the insinuation. It was printed in 1715, a year after publication of the final version of *The Rape of the Lock,* and purports to be an analysis of it. The "author", one "Esdras Barnivelt, Apothecary", asserts that the poem is a political allegory satirizing the Tory Ministry and the events which led up to the Barrier Treaty, and covertly advocating Roman Catholicism. There are hints throughout that the author may be a persona created by a writer who has his tongue in his cheek, but they are only hints. The second edition of the "Treatise" is prefaced by a number of doggerel poems celebrating the "author" and allegedly written "by the most Eminent Political Wits of the Age".[7] Bad verses were not uncommon of course, but the quality of these, and the unfamiliarity of the names of the "Eminent Political Wits" would give the perceptive reader a clue. Within the *Key* itself, the absurdity of some of the comments Barnivelt makes, and the outrageous distortions of the text of *The Rape of the Lock* he uses to "prove" his charges against Pope, are sufficient to gradually arouse the reader's suspicions at one point or another.

On the other hand, if there is no shock at all, or any external indication of insinuation, the satire is almost certain to be misread. Pope's *Guardian* essay Number 40 was taken by two of his early biographers to have been aimed at Pope himself and his Horatian epistle addressed "To Augustus" accepted by some as a panegyric upon George II. The first edition of Samuel Butler's *The Fair Haven* was taken quite seriously by orthodox churchmen. Edward Weeks tells us that John Marquand's *The Late George Apley* was read quite literally by some "proper Bostonians" who "appeared at the Boston Museum of Fine Arts on Sunday afternoon asking to be shown the 'Apley Bronzes' ".[8] Doubtless a number of satires exist which have never been read in the way the author intended simply because the fact he was insinuating was never made clear.

Probably the most famous example of general misreading is Defoe's *The Shortest Way with the Dissenters (1702)*. The tract was published anonymously at the height of the controversy over Occasional Conformity. Defoe, a Dissenter himself, assumed the persona of a fanatical

---

[7]   The title-page to the second edition is reproduced in *The Prose Works of Alexander Pope*, ed. Norman Ault (Oxford, 1936), I, 173.

[8]   "John P. Marquand", *Harper's* (October, 1960), p. 75.

High Church Tory and argued the Dissenters were a menace to the realm and that the most extreme measures should be taken against them:

'Tis high time then for the Friends of the Church of *England,* to think of Building up, and Establishing her, in such a manner, that she may be no more Invaded by Foreigners, nor Divided by Factions, Schisms, and Error.

If this cou'd be done by gentle and easy Methods, I shou'd be glad, but the Wound is coroded, the Vitals begin to mortifie, and nothing but Amputation of Members can compleat the Cure; all the ways of Tenderness and Compassion, all perswasive Arguments have been made use of in vain.

. . . *Alas the Church of England!* What with Popery on one Hand, and Schismaticks on the other; how has she been Crucify'd between two Thieves.

Now, *let us Crucifie the Thieves.* Let her Foundations be establish'd upon the Destruction of her Enemies: The Doors of Mercy being always open to the returning Part of the deluded People: let the Obstinate be rul'd with the Rod of Iron.[9]

Defoe's persona outdoes fanatics like his contemporary Henry Sacheverell, but making distinctions between degrees of fanaticism is more easily done in the study than in streets and assemblies when passions run high. Perhaps inevitably, the tract was misread, and when its true import was discovered Defoe was pilloried and imprisoned. The very fact that the tract was misread may have had something to do with the severity with which the author was punished.[10]

Doubtless Ian Watt is right in concluding that Defoe was unable to step off the proper distance between himself and his character – that instead of creating a satiric persona he impersonated a High Church Tory all too successfully.[11] Since Defoe gave his readers no unmistakable indication that he wanted the tract to be read from a different perspective than the persona's own – there is no shock, in other words – contemporary misreading was inevitable.

The more extreme forms of satiric shock might seem to have some affinities with the feelings of outrage or disgust produced by some

---

[9]   *Novels and Selected Writings,* XIV, 131-133.
[10]   Perhaps during difficult times the authorities may be particularly sensitive to indirect satire. François Lacheval writes that during the last days of the Nazi regime in Berlin before it fell to the Russians in World War II "A critical reflection on the regime or on the conduct of the war reported to the police involved imprisonment at least; if you had insidiously given it the appearance of eulogy (*Heimtücke*), the punishment might be capital." "Last Days of Berlin", in *The Golden Horizon,* p. 114.
[11]   *The Rise of the Novel* (Berkeley and Los Angeles, 1959), p. 126.

direct satires. Satiric shock may also seem analogous to the shocked
revulsion produced by Swift's description of the microscopic view of the
human body in Part II of *Gulliver's Travels,* of the bestiality of the
Yahoos in Part IV. Pope arouses similar feelings with the "Hogs of
Westphaly" passage in *Epilogue to the Satires, Dialogue II* (11. 171-
180) as does William Golding in the climactic chapters of *Lord of the
Flies* when the boys on his desert island become little more than
preying animals. Yet though all these incidents do indeed shock the
reader, they are used to intensify, to drive home unmistakably and
unforgettably a specific satiric point for which the writer of the satire
has already prepared his reader. They emphasize, in other words, rather
than originate the satiric effect.

The general device of surprising the reader is of course a venerable
and familiar rhetorical tactic. A writer working in any genre may violate his reader's expectations and break decorum or convention to seize
attention and arouse curiosity. The satirist wants to do these things,
but he usually wants to do more than merely surprise.

His purpose varies from satire to satire. Swift, for example, in *A
Modest Proposal,* uses shock to establish the metaphor of people
EATING people, a metaphor which informs the entire work. T. S. Eliot
in *The Love Song of J. Alfred Prufrock* shocks us with an image: ". . . the
evening is spread out against the sky/ Like a patient etherized upon a
table"[12] (an image doubtless more shocking to a contemporary reader
than to us who have been educated by Mr. Eliot and his colleagues).
The image implies what is to follow: Prufrock is to be opened, probed,
dissected. Evelyn Waugh in *The Loved One* tricks us into accepting a
description on false premises, yet having accepted it, we are at least
partially prepared for the next step – recognizing that Southern California not only appears to be but in fact is a wasteland inhabited by
barbarians. Nathanael West's *Miss Lonelyhearts* begins with the shock
embodied in the parody of the *Anima Christi.* The parody not only
alerts us to the possibility that the novel may be one which will demand
more than a merely literal reading, its bitter parody appropriately intro-
duces us to the lonely torment of that modern Christ, Miss Lonelyhearts himself.

Robert Burns' *Holy Willie's Prayer*, another example, begins with a
shock which helps to set up a number of satiric points. Burns calls the
poem "Willie's Prayer", uses Pope's line "And send the Godly in a pet
to pray–" as an epigraph and in the argument (often printed with the

[12]   *Collected Poems, 1909-1935* (New York, 1936), p. 11.

poem) describes Willie as a "rather Oldish bachelor Elder" famed for "polemical Chattering, which ends in tippling Orthodoxy, for that Spiritualized Bawdry which refines to Liquorish Devotion". The diminutive, "Willie", the suggestion of peevishness in the epigraph and the description of Willie in the argument – none of these really prepares us for the sublime arrogance of the opening stanzas:

> O Thou, that in the Heavens does dwell,
> Wha, as it pleases best Thysel,
> Sends ane to Heaven an' ten to Hell,
>   A' for Thy glory,
> And no for onie guid or ill
>   They've done before Thee!
> I bless and praise Thy matchless might,
> When thousands Thou hast left in night,
> That I am here before Thy sight,
>   For gifts an' grace
> A burning and a shining light
>   To a' this place.[13]

The reader is shocked, not only by the stark statement of the Calvinist doctrine of "election", but by Willie's assumption that he is one of the favored chosen by God as an example to all. Willie's arrogance, here so forcibly established, does more than merely surprise us; it deepens the irony of his confession that he is "fash'd wi' fleshly lust" (stanza 6) and helps prepare us for the superb explanation of why God has afflicted him with lust:

> Maybe Thou lets this fleshy thorn
> Buffet Thy servant e'en and morn,
> Lest he owre proud and high should turn,
>   That he's sae gifted:
> If sae, Thy hand maun e'en be borne,
> Until Thou lift it.
>
>   (stanza 9)

He echoes the second epistle to the Corinthians – equates St. Paul's "thorn in the flesh" (II Cor. 12:7) with his own tumbles in the hay. Arrogance could scarcely be carried further.

In the remaining seven stanzas of the poem Willie rains maledictions upon Gavin Hamilton, Robert Aiken, and the Presbytery of Ayr for humiliating him; he accuses Hamilton of drinking, swearing, and playing at cards. But his own arrogance has so conditioned our responses

[13] *The Poems of Robert Burns and Selected Letters*, ed. Anthony Hepburn (London and Glasgow, 1959), p. 50.

that his accusations serve to praise, rather than condemn. Our awareness of the contradiction in Willie's character heightened, his request that God curse Hamilton's "basket and his store,/Kail an' potatoes!" (stanza 12) and his prayer that the Lord make him "shine" for "grace an' gear" (16) sharpens the implied condemnation of Willie's sense of values, and his admission that at the session he "stood sweatin, shakin,/ An 'p-'d dread" (14) becomes a more ludicrous picture of abject fear.

The satiric shock with which the poem begins is essential to its effect, for the poem is built upon a shocking contrast – a contrast between lofty conceit and pretty desire for vengeance, and between Willie's sublime, blind arrogance, and his ridiculous attempt to con God into taking his side in a petty squabble. The emphasis placed upon arrogance by the shock throws another aspect of the poem into bold relief. The first stanzas are a strikingly extreme statement, not of Willie's credo alone, but of Calvinist beliefs in general. The extreme statement of Calvinist position emphasizes the larger implications of the poem – Holy Willie's Prayer is not only one of the great satiric portraits in English literature, it is implicitly a condemnation of Calvinist theology. Thus it is not only a lampoon, but a great general satire as well.

Shock in all of the satires just mentioned occurs early enough to enable the reader to adjust his set before he has read far into the work. If the shock is delayed, the satirist risks dissipating a good part of the satiric effect, for he cannot be sure the reader will take the trouble to turn back and begin all over again. In *Erewhon,* one long satire in which the shock does not come early, the loss is not a great one since the early parts of the novel are chiefly straightforward narrative. But this is unusual. Most satires in which shock is delayed are short. E. E. Cummings, in his superbly economical "come, gaze with me upon this dome", needs only twenty lines to embody the whole turn-of-the-century romantic view of a departure for war before the last stanza undercuts its smug naïveteé:

> much kissed, by loving relatives
> well fed, and fully photographed
> the son of man goes forth to war
> with trumpets clap and syphilis[14]

Swift used the same tactic in *A Description of a City Shower,* which

---

[14]   *The Oxford Book of American Verse*, ed. F. O. Matthiessen (New York, 1950), p. 933.

ends with the shock of recognizable parody in the last three lines. The effect is to suggest a reinterpretation of the poem, an apparently "realistic" description of London before and during a rainfall. Alerted by the shock, we may recognize that the poem is a satiric commentary upon conventional descriptive poems, whether or not we are willing to follow the lead of a modern critic who argues that the poem is "an oblique denunciation of cathartic doom upon the corruption of the city".[15] Shirley Jackson's *The Lottery* ends with the shocking revelation of the savage purpose of a ceremonial drawing of lots in an apparently typical small town. Doubtless most of us have become more and more uneasy as we read the story – there are too many details whose import we do not understand. But the final disclosure that the purpose of the lottery is to select a human victim for ritual murder reveals in a flash the primitive, pagan impulses which, Miss Jackson insinuates, lie just below the surface of apparently civilized modern men.

As I have suggested above, one way of looking at satiric shock is to see it as an attempt to warn the reader that the author, or his persona, is insinuating, to suggest that a literal reading will not do. The shock may be overlooked, misconstrued, or even if it is properly construed, not be followed by perfect comprehension of every nuance of the satire which embodies it.[16] But the reader has been alerted, and the writer of the satire may at least hope that once aware of the general drift the reader will be responsive to finer strokes of insinuation. Thus the satirist attempts to "make" the reader in the sense of the word that Henry James suggests. In *The Rhetoric of Fiction*, Wayne Booth quotes the novelist and explains the term as James uses it:

The true value of forcing the reader to decipher lies in what such activity does to his attitude toward the story and its author. In his early *Atlantic Monthly* review from which I have already quoted James on the art of "making the reader", his whole emphasis is on this one aspect. "When he makes him well, that is makes him interested, then the reader does quite half the labor." James is not thinking here simply of giving the reader a sense of his own cleverness. He is making his readers by forcing them onto a level of alertness that will allow for his most subtle effects.[17]

[15]   Brendan O Hehir, "Meaning of Swift's 'Description of a City Shower' ", *ELH*, XXVII (1960), 206.
[16]   See Wayne C. Booth's lucid discussion "Troubles with Irony in Earlier Literature", in *The Rhetoric of Fiction* (Chicago and London, 1961), pp. 316-323. He discusses *Jonathan Wild, The Shortest Way with the Dissenters, A Modest Proposal, Gulliver's Travels*, and *Barry Lyndon*, all satires in the sense I am using the term, as well as other, non-satiric works.
[17]   Booth, "Troubles", p. 302. He notes that the quotation from James is from *The Atlantic Monthly* (October, 1866), p. 485.

The shock warns the reader of insinuation and helps force him to a level of alertness that will allow the satirist's tactics to have their full effect – and I suspect that there is frequently another effect as well. When the reader realizes he has been misled and must re-adjust his set, he is in a sense an object of the satire, for he has been convicted of a lack of perception. Having been fooled himself he is all the more willing to see others, or their ideas, ridiculed. He begins to become less a mere reader, more an active cooperator with the satirist. He begins the process by which both reader and satirist together create, explore, and share the unique point of view which is the basis of any good satire. The reader becomes, in short, one of the members of the coterie which is the audience of satire.

IV

SATIRIC FORMS, PARODIES, AND PATTERNS

It is often remarked that English satire is protean. It seems to have no characteristic forms, much less invariable ones. As the most cursory glance through an anthology of satire will make clear, satires have been written in the forms of odes, elegies, love-songs, pastoral ballads, heroic poems. They have taken the forms of anecdotes, biographies, political pamphlets, dedications, tales, and reviews. Satiric forms range from the most sacred – saint's lives, sermons, prayers – to the most secular – "How-to-do-it" manuals, guide-books, and business letters. And a list like this could be lengthened almost indefinitely.

The very length of such a list, and the variety of forms included in it, suggest that two generalizations may not be out of order. We may argue, first of all, that satire seems to have no distinctive forms of its own, since all the forms mentioned above are used in non-satiric works, and the satirist has merely adapted them for his own use. If this is so, a second generalization seems reasonable. If satire invariably adapts forms, this very adaptive quality is a most distinctive hallmark of satire, one which clearly sets it off from other kinds of literature. Moreover, the forms the satirist chooses to adapt are not chosen at random; they are directly related to the object of the aggression itself – in fact, can be part of the tactics. In other words the satirist frequently adopts a certain kind of structure in the expectation that the reader will recognize it, and that he can use the reader's recognition as one of the strands of the web of insinuation which is the basis of the satire.

Two popular forms will exemplify some of the ways in which forms may be adapted. They might be called the "project" and the "discovery".[1] The project or scheme is usually a proposal which puts into concrete form ideas, tendencies and conditions the satirist wants to

---

[1] The terms are used in Ricardo Quintana's important essay, "Situational Satire: A Commentary on the Method of Swift", *University of Toronto Quarterly*, XVII (1948), 130-136, to which I am indebted for some of the ideas in this chapter.

attack. It frequently begins with a statement of the conditions which make the scheme necessary or desirable, continues with a sketch of the desirable results which the project will lead to, and ends with a request for action. However, any of these parts may be subordinated, omitted, or much more fully developed than the others so long as the essence of the proposal is maintained. Sometimes the project is merely a brief suggestion whose consequences are left to the reader's imagination. Or, instead of merely a request for action, we have a detailed working-out of the consequences of the proposal. In cases like these most of the satire may be a dramatiza⁺on in detail of the implications of the project. The project is frequently used to attack the individuals who advance the scheme, the audience to which it is addressed, or the conditions which make such a scheme "reasonable" or possible. The projector himself may be one of the objects of the satire, though in projects advanced by an ingénu – an innocent, or the victim of circumstances – he escapes all or most of the blame.

The speaker in *A Modest Proposal* and Mr. Higgs in *Erewhon* are both projectors. The project in *A Modest Proposal* is used primarily to focus attention upon the people and the conditions which make the scheme "reasonable". The satire embodied in Mr. Higgs' proposal is chiefly directed at his audience – "Christians" who are willing to countenance the use of their religion as a cover for the exploitation of native peoples on the pretext of evangelizing them.

The projects in these two satires, like the projected Academy of Wits in the preface to *A Tale of a Tub,* remain in the form of proposals. Other projects are put into action and the whole satire, or a considerable portion of it, may be a description of a detailed working-out of the scheme. The Eden Land Corporation project, a scheme for settling the wilderness of America in which Martin Chuzzlewit and Mark Tapley participate, is not only described, its melancholy effect upon those who are deluded by the project is shown in considerable detail. Saki's *Filboid Studge, the Story of a Mouse that Helped* is based upon a project suggested by an ingénu; much of the education of Martinus Scriblerus is a type of project; and a good deal of the action in *Animal Farm* is the result of projects put into motion. (The episode of the building of the windmill reminds us of a similar project in Part III of *Gulliver's Travels,* which may have suggested it.) Orwell's "Newspeak" in *Nineteen Eighty Four* is essentially a project, too; it is described in action in the body of the novel and its theory discussed in an appendix. Some of the episodes in *Huckleberry Finn* involve shady projects initiated by the King and the Duke; a good part of H. G. Wells' *Tono-Bungay* is based upon a business project; and the episodes in Herman Melville's *The Confidence-Man* are virtually one project after another. As many of these references suggest, projects of one kind or another are common in satires dealing with confidence-men, the underworld, or the business world.

The "discovery" is a satiric form used to satirize seekers after certain kinds of knowledge, usually "scientific" knowledge of one kind or another. The object of the satire may be either the seekers themselves, as in Part III of *Gulliver's Travels* and in the elder Samuel Butler's *The Elephant in the Moon* and *Satyr on the Royal Society,* or both the seekers AND the initiators of investigations, like Dr. Obispo and Jo Stoyte in Aldous Huxley's *After Many a Summer* and the priest and the alchemist in *The Canon's Yeoman's Tale.*

Like the project, with which it has some obvious affinities, the discovery may be only a proposal, in which case the satirist is likely to treat it rather cursorily. But if it is treated at length – its germination, growth, and final flowering detailed – it may form the basis of an extended satiric episode, or even a whole work. *Brave New World,* like many satiric works about the future, is full of discoveries – methods for breeding test-tube babies, chemical tablets which produce feelings of well-being – and *After Many a Summer* contains an extended account of the search for and discovery of an extract from the intestines of carp which will extend the span of human life. Discoveries, as one might expect, occur most frequently during periods like the eighteenth and twentieth centuries when science was most active and when its methods and ultimate ends were most suspect.

As I mentioned above, all of these forms occur in non-satire as well as satire. Some of them, moreover, are recognizably similar to specific non-satiric works. *A Modest Proposal* is identical in structure to certain non-satiric economic tracts whose authors had argued that people were the real wealth of a country. The similarity is not fortuitous; Swift expected that his original readers would recognize the similarity and recognize also that the similarities in structure but difference in content and tone would insinuate the futility of panaceas which did not take the condition of one specific country, Ireland, into account. In other words, the structure of *A Modest Proposal* is itself one of the tactics of insinuation. Mr. Higgs' project for settling the natives of Erewhon in Queensland as laborers in the sugar plantations is similar to other schemes for settling heathens in undeveloped countries, and the Eden Land Corporation bears a recognizable affinity to certain plans for selling plots of wilderness land to other uninformed, but hopeful, pioneers. In both cases the hypocrisy of the promoters of such projects seems to be the chief object of the satire. In both cases the satirist insinuates that the idealistic professions of the promoters – to spread the Gospel in one case, to promote the dignity of man in the other – are merely convenient covers for selfish motives.

The structures of these satiric projects have certain similarities, as I have said, to specific non-satiric projects. They also have similarities to a very much larger group of non-satiric projects which, whatever their specific ends, are based upon optimism and are at least professedly idealistic. Since so many projects are optimistic and idealistic, the very structure of a project may be said to carry a faint aura of optimism and idealism. Thus if the satirist chooses the form of a project to contain his satiric attack, he can usually count upon at least a mild derogatory insinuation which is the result of a contrast between the associations carried by the structure and the less optimistic, less idealistic matter which he has put into it.[2]

The same general point might be made about the "discovery". The form is normally used to describe the processes by which new scientific facts are discovered, facts which will enable man to better understand the natural world, to ameliorate conditions of human life, or to prolong it. Implicit in the announcement of discoveries like these are certain assumptions – the disinterestedness of the seekers for new knowledge, for instance, or their wisdom in discovering things that have eluded others, or the value of such knowledge for its own sake. A satirist then may use these associations to insinuate, or to reinforce an insinuation that discoveries may be based upon less worthy assumptions, that the motives of some seekers for knowledge may be self-seeking ones, or even that the ends of certain kinds of scientific investigations are pernicious or blameworthy.

We needn't of course assume two satires with similar structures must be aimed at precisely the same targets, for the structure is merely a point of departure and the direction of the aggression may be profoundly modified by the other tactics the satirist uses. *A Modest Proposal*, for example, is aimed primarily at those responsible for conditions in Ireland which make Swift's projector's proposal "reasonable". Butler's target seems to be primarily the hypocrisy of certain

[2] In *A Modest Proposal*, Swift also plays upon the contrast between the pejorative and non-pejorative contemporary meaning of "projector".

kinds of Christians. Dickens is mainly interested in exposing hypo-critical greed, one of whose manifestations happens to be a bunco scheme. However it is clear that though the precise object of the satire may vary, the adapted structure may be one of the primary insinuating tactics and may provide an important clue to at least some of the targets of the aggression.

The fact that many satirists choose forms which will carry part of the burden of insinuation is suggestive, for it points to the possibility that we can recognize at least some kind of organizing principle in the welter of forms that the satirist uses. We can hardly say that all forms are chosen on this principle, but it is clear that certain kinds of structures are intended to work as a satiric tactic. The satirist expects that the reader will recognize them and the associations they carry, even though he may not refer to them directly; and he can use the reader's recognition to establish, or support, the web of insinuation which embodies the satiric aggression.

Though I have not used the word thus far, satiric adaptations of structure are a form of parody, but "parody" in a more wide-ranging sense than we are likely to use the word today. Samuel Johnson defined it as the seventeenth and eighteenth centuries understood it: "A kind of writing, in which the words of an author or his thoughts are taken, and by a slight change adapted to some new purpose." Parody in his sense allows for the possibility that the adaptation may be used for a purpose OTHER THAN criticism of the original. This kind of parody is a basic satiric tactic. It is perhaps most familiar in satires written during the seventeenth and eighteenth centuries, but is very frequently found also in satires of all periods. The modern sense of the word, however, is too limited to cover the tactic adequately, for we generally use the word to mean parody OF some specific literary work. Parody in this sense is an imitation, exaggeration and distortion of the style and sometimes the structure of a given work, or writer, or even school of writers, and the object of the parody is it, or him, or them. It is usually a kind of literary criticism, frequently a very subtle and penetrating one. As William Van O'Connor reminds us, parody can make us "see, or better... *experience* the nature of a style and subject, and their excesses".[3] Parodies like *Shamela,* like those in Max Beerbohm's *A Christmas Garland,* like Wolcott Gibbs's famous profile of Henry Luce, "*Time ... Fortune ... Life ... Luce", to* name only a few familiar ones, are properly a part of satire. Many

[3] "Parody as Criticism", *College English*, XXV (1964), 241.

parodies stand in relation to satire much like the lampoon. That is, they are attacks upon specific literary works, as the lampoon is an attack upon a specific individual. Often there is a carry-over, and the parody may not only be an attack upon a specific work by a given author, but upon his other works, or upon the whole literary movement of which he is a part. *Northanger Abbey,* for instance, whatever its references to specific works, parodies the whole school of Gothic novels, and Chaucer's *Sir Thopas* is aimed at the conventions, style and subjects of a large group of medieval metrical romancers.

Since the overlapping meanings of the word are likely to be confusing, I should like to restrict "parody" to its modern sense – that is, an imitation and alteration or distortion of the style or structure of an original for the purpose of criticizing it – and use "pattern" to denote any adaptation of an original for satiric purposes when the chief purpose is not parody. A pattern may adapt the language of its original, its structure or its characters. Adaptations of language we shall want to consider later and need only touch lightly here. Adaptations of structure are our main concern, but since these can hardly be separated from certain kinds of characters who are involved in the structure, in many instances we shall have to consider them together.

A pattern generally seems to be adapted for one of two reasons. It may, first of all, be adapted to insinuate a similarity between an original and the object of the satire, the similarity suggesting something blameworthy about the object of the satire. In Chaucer's portrait of the Prioress nine lines are devoted to a description of the nun's manners at table:

> At mete wel ytaught was she with alle:
> She leet no morsel from hir lippes falle,
> Ne wette hir fyngres in hir sauce depe;
> Wel koude she carie a morsel and wel kepe
> That no drope ne fille upon hire brest.
> In curteisie was set ful muchel hir lest.
> Hir over-lippe wyped she so clene
> That in hir coppe ther was no ferthyng sene
> Of grece, whan she dronken hadde hir draughte.
> Ful semely after hir mete she raughte.
>   (127-136)

The nun's manners match, detail for detail, those advocated by the old Duenna in *The Romance of the Rose,* who is advising fashionable young ladies:

She should not wet her fingers in the sauce
Beyond the joint, nor soil her lips with soup,
With garlic, or fat meat; nor pile a heap
Of food and then convey it to her mouth.
With tips of fingers she should handle bits
That she should dip in sauce, white, yellow, or green,
And very carefully the mouthful lift,
That on her breast no bit of pepper falls,
Or soup or gravy. Then so gracefully
She should her goblet quaff that not a drop
She spills upon her clothes, for far too rude
Or gluttonous men might consider her
If they should see such accident occur.
The common cup should not approach her lips
While yet there is some food within her chops;
And ere she drinks she wipes her mouth so clean
That on her lips no speck of grease adheres,
At least not on her upper lip, for then
Globules of it might float upon the wine,
Which would be most disgusting and not neat.[4]

(101-120)

The passage from *The Romance of the Rose* has obviously not
only suggested a structure for Chaucer's passage; the structure itself
is one of the insinuating tactics. The reader who remembers this
section of *The Romance of the Rose* will recall also that the manners
the Duenna describes are intended to win the favorable attention of
a lover and respond to Chaucer's insinuation that there is a touch too
much of the worldly woman in the Prioress.

A second kind of adapted pattern is used to insinuate a difference
between something outside the satire and something within it. That is,
a pattern which is associated with certain kinds of values, or certain
kinds of attitudes – we can call both "norms" for the sake of simplicity – is used in such a way that a contrast is set up between the
norms of the original and the norms of the object of the satire. The
norms associated with the original may be more exalted than those
in the satire, or merely different. Whichever the case, they will serve
the satirist's purpose if the EFFECT of the contrast is to reveal something blameworthy about the object of the satire.

Two such patterns, both short enough to conveniently illustrate the
point, occur in the first canto of *The Rape of the Lock:*

[4] Guillaume de Lorris and Jean de Meun, *The Romance of the Rose,* trans.
Harry W. Robbins and edited with an introduction by Charles W. Dunn (New
York, 1962), p. 280.

And now, unveil'd, the *Toilet* stands display'd,
Each Silver Vase in mystic Order laid.
First, rob'd in White, the Nymph intent adores
With Head uncover'd, the *Cosmetic* Pow'rs.
A heav'nly Image in the Glass appears,
To that she bends, to that her Eyes she rears;
Th' inferior Priestess, at her Altar's side,
Trembling, begins the sacred Rites of Pride.[5]

(I, 121-128)

Belinda's actions here are patterned upon the consecration of the Mass. She adores the cosmetic powers symbolized by the silver vases and bends to the image of her own fair self in the mirror. The contrasts between original and adapted pattern makes the author's point more effective than any direct statement could.

A few lines later we see Belinda being made up before she sallies forth for the day:

Now awful Beauty puts on all its Arms;
The Fair each moment rises in her Charms,
Repairs her Smiles, awakens ev'ry Grace,
And calls forth all the Wonders of her Face;
Sees by Degrees a purer Blush arise,
And keener Lightnings quicken in her Eyes.

(I, 139-144)

The pattern here of course is the arming of the epic hero; the adaptation has only to be noted for the insinuation to be appreciated.

Yet, though perhaps the most obvious effect of the patterns used in these passages is to score points against Belinda – and by extension contemporary belles – the total effect is not solely to stress Belinda's blameworthiness. The adapted patterns are incongruous; but they are *con*gruous, too. Not only these passages, but the poem as a whole implies that there is something genuinely awe-inspiring and goddess-like about Belinda. Her adoration of her own image has its counterpart in the homage others pay her. The society she lives in is neither genuinely religious nor heroic and the homage and honor paid to beauty are to some extent the equivalent of the homage paid to God and the honor paid to heroes in other societies. Thus the satire on Belinda is qualified by a genuine tribute the writer of the poem pays her, but this very tribute insinuates something blameworthy about the society in which she lives. Perhaps we should add a third effect to the two mentioned above. The pattern may not only insinuate a compari-

---

[5] *The Poems of Alexander Pope*, The Twickenham Edition, ed. John Butt *et al.*, 3rd ed. (London and New Haven, 1939-61), II, 155.

son or contrast, the effect of which is to suggest blameworthiness, it may insinuate both at the same time, and in so doing reveal an extra dimension of the satire.

Frequently a satiric pattern may be only one of a number of threads in a work made up of a complex mixture of satiric and non-satiric material. Patterns like this are frequently found in modern novels where they may insinuate a satiric meaning in a work which is only partly satiric, or blend with a complicated mixture of other satiric patterns or tactics. Ivor Claire in Evelyn Waugh's *Officers and Gentlemen* is the very model of a foppish English gentleman – a cool, aloof, non-conformist called to serve his country in a desperate emergency. He recalls the whole tradition, embodied in a hundred light novels, of the British amateur who outrages orthodoxy but when the going is toughest defeats the enemies of King and country with a combination of ingenuity, luck, and typical English pluck. Claire fits the pattern perfectly until the moment of supreme testing when he cracks and deserts in the face of the enemy. His behavior and character until the moment of desertion recall the pattern; his desertion and the reasons for it are criticism of its falseness. His desertion does more than this. It undermines romantic illusion about a certain kind of English character, and in the process undermines some illusions about the kind of war English "officers and gentlemen" are called upon to fight in the modern world.

A pattern may not only be used for a local effect within a satiric work; it may suggest structure and characterization for the whole. *Gulliver's Travels* is patterned upon a whole genre of voyage literature; Gulliver himself has some recognizable similarities to the heroes of such voyages, and his laconic, matter-of-fact descriptions frequently echo their similar accounts of the wonders they have seen. Some of the characters and many of the incidents of the plot of William Golding's *Lord of the Flies* recall Robert Michael Ballantyne's popular nineteenth century novel *The Coral Island*. Swift's pattern reminds his reader of the idyllic view of human nature unspoiled by contact with civilized man which is frequently found in the travel books. *Gulliver's Travels* is at any rate partly a commentary upon that idealized conception of unspoiled humanity. Golding's point is similar. His English schoolboys who revert to savagery in the midst of unspoiled nature not only contrast with Ballantyne's heroes but implicitly undercut the optimistic view of human nature at the core of *The Coral Island*.[6]

[6] See Carl Niemeyer, "The Coral Island Revisited", *College English*, XXII (1961), 241-245, for a useful summary of *The Coral Island*.

I argued above that pattern and parody were related but essentially distinct kinds of adaptations of originals since they are used for different purposes. However, as the examples cited above make clear, a pattern is often tinged with parody. There is obviously an element of parody in both *Gulliver's Travels* and *Lord of the Flies,* but the chief purpose of the adaptations is to attack larger targets than the absurdities of a group of travel writers, in Swift's case, or a largely forgotten nineteenth century novel, in Golding's. Their originals have furnished recognizable patterns, but Swift and Golding are after more important game. On the other hand, Pope's adaptation of the consecration of the Mass and of the arming of the epic hero to satirize Belinda and her society do not seem to be parodies of either the religious service or the epic convention. Pope uses these structures, but the insinuation is not aimed at them.

As these examples will also suggest, patterns differ widely in the closeness of their relationship to the original. In Chaucer's portrait of the Prioress the parallel with *The Romance of the Rose* is close and exact. In some of the other examples the details vary from those of the original, or they have been re-arranged – Pope has varied the details of the consecration, for example. In some cases the original survives only as a skeleton and new flesh is provided by the satirist. In E. E. Cummings' POEM, OR BEAUTY HURTS MR. VINAL fragments of *America the Beautiful* are interspersed with advertising slogans, product names, authorial comment:

> take it from me kiddo
> believe me
> my country, 'tis of
>
> you, land of the Cluett
> Shirt Boston Garter and Spearmint
> Girl With The Wrigley Eyes (of you
> land of the Arrow Ide
> and Earl &
> Wilson
> Collars) of you i
> sing: land of Abraham Lincoln and Lydia E. Pinkham,
> land above all of Just Add Hot Water And Serve –
> from every B. V. D.
>
> let freedom ring[7]

---

[7]   *The Oxford Book of American Verse*, p. 926.

The framework here is just enough to provide a structure for the poem and to suggest points of reference for Cummings' attack, not just upon the patriotic song alone, but the banality, materialism and intellectual poverty of American life which the song ignores.

In patterns based not on a single original but upon forms found in a number of works, very exact parallels are usually not possible. A general resemblance will suffice. Once the general resemblance is established, however, variations may be important clues to the interpretation of the satire as is, for instance, Ivor Claire's break with his pattern. Variations or breaks with pattern may surprise or shock the reader and thus alert him to the insinuation which is the basis of the whole work.

We might distinguish three groupings of patterns upon the basis of the kinds of originals from which the patterns are adapted. First, there are patterns based upon specific literary originals. Second, there are patterns adapted from originals found in a number of literary works, the structures common to the works belonging to a non-satiric genre, for example. Finally, we might distinguish patterns adapted not from works of literature at all, but from recognizable non-literary structures.

Pope's *Peri Bathous,* or *Of the Art of Sinking in Poetry* is a good example of the first kind of pattern. Its pattern is of course adapted from Longinus' *Peri Hupsous,* or *On the Sublime.* Though satires in this first group are tinged with parody, were it not obvious in *Peri Bathous* itself there is ample outside evidence that Pope had the highest regard for Longinus. *Peri Bathous* furnished a structure which Pope's audience would recognize. Not only would they recognize the pattern of *Peri Bathous,* they would associate it with a certain kind of writing which contrasted strongly with the sorts of writing contemporary poetasters – the objects of the satire – were doing. Thus the pattern not only furnished a structure and suggested a kind of language appropriate for Pope's purpose, it implied a standard of values by which the objects of the satire could be judged.

Although the patterns of the satires in the first group are based upon specific literary originals, a close knowledge of the original may or may not be essential to an understanding of the general satiric implications of the work. A good deal depends upon the tone and the other tactics of the individual satire. A knowledge of Golding's original in *Lord of the Flies* is not absolutely essential to an understanding of its general meaning for instance. Doubtless most American readers, at any rate, have not read *The Coral Island,* and many have never heard of it and thus miss even the general implications of the pattern. Recognizing the original, however, sharpens the satiric impact of the novel and brings some of the objects of the satire into bolder relief. On the other hand, the pattern upon which Chaucer has based his description of the Prioress' manners is much more crucial to the satiric effect of the portrait. A knowledge of the parallel in *The Romance of the Rose* makes it clear that what might seem to be incidental details are in fact carefully calculated to insinuate a fault. It would seem that the subtler the satire or the closer the satire is to a non-satiric form, the more important becomes an understanding of the original from which the satiric pattern has been adapted.

Other satires which belong to this group include such apparently disparate works as Skelton's *The Bowge of Court,* Herman Melville's *The Confidence Man,* and Katherine Anne Porter's *Ship of Fools,* all of which are patterned upon Sebastian Brant's *The Ship of Fools;*[8] Swift's *A Description of a City Shower,* patterned upon a passage in Virgil's *Georgics;* Dryden's *Absalom and Achitophel*; many of James Joyce's works (*Ulysses* of course is the most familiar example; it uses a number of adapted patterns including the Hell, Purgatory, Heaven pattern of *The Divine Comedy* which is used also in the short-story "Grace" and *A Portrait of the Artist*);[9] and Oliver Jensen's amusing exercise in *Eisenhowerese,* the Gettysburg address as General Eisenhower might have written it. And, since this group of patterns stands closest to parody as we have defined it above, perhaps we should include the large number of parodies like Byron's *The Vision of Judgment* whose objects range beyond merely literary criticism.

A second group of satires is based upon patterns which are literary, or have frequently been used in literary works, but are intended to suggest not single works but a whole genre. Thus the insinuation carried by the pattern is likely to be less sharp and specific, but to be more adaptable. The usual effect is to play a form which has been identified with a certain kind of literary content and certain characteristic attitudes against the object of the satire. In the elder Samuel Butler's *To the Happy Memory of the Most Reknowned Du-Val: A Pindaric Ode,* for example, the pattern of the English adaptation of the Pindaric ode, a form originally devoted to the celebration of gods or heroes, is used

---

[8]   There is a good discussion of this aspect of *The Bowge of Court* in A. R. Heiserman, *Skelton and Satire* (Chicago, 1961), p. 39.
[9]   See the useful discussions of these works of Joyce in William York Tindall, *A Reader's Guide to James Joyce* (New York, 1959).

to "glorify" the exploits of a well-known highwayman. A good part of the effect depends upon the reader's recognition of the incongruity (and doubtless the minor *congruity*) of pattern and the matter it contains.

This group is quite a large one for it includes most "mock-heroic" works as well as mock-elegies, odes, songs, pastorals, reviews, sermons, obituaries and the like. The qualifying "mock" is unfortunate, for it is likely to suggest that these mock-genres are primarily intended to ridicule the non-satiric works upon which they are patterned. Mocking the epic, critics have traditionally averred, is part of the intention of the mock-epic. Recent critics have tended to deny or minimize this view. The amount of satire upon the epic itself in satires like *Mac Flecknoe, The Rape of the Lock, The Dunciad* really seems minimal. What is beyond question is that when the idea of the epic was alive its pattern was ideally suited to playing pattern against content and this sufficiently accounts for its popularity in satire. Like the vogue of other satiric patterns, the vogue of the mock-heroic is closely bound up with interest in the form as a non-satiric vehicle.

Neither the novel nor the short story is sufficiently identified with a certain kind of subject matter to make it a useful pattern, but frequently identifiable patterns are used within them. I have already mentioned *Gulliver's Travels* and *Erewhon,* patterned upon voyage and travel literature, and a pattern used in Evelyn Waugh's *Officers and Gentlemen.* We might also include novels like Nathanael West's *The Dream Life of Balso Snell,* Ronald Firbank's *The Flower Beneath the Foot,* and Norman's Douglas' *South Wind,* all of which have sections patterned upon the saint's life; and F. Scott Fitzgerald's *The Great Gatsby,*[10] William Faulkner's *The Hamlet,* and West's *A Cool Million,* the exploits of whose heroes are patterned upon those of the typical Horatio Alger hero.

A third kind of pattern imitates something found in life – or at least in a non-literary source. It may be based upon a recognizable sequence of events like a coronation, whose pattern is adapted in *Mac Flecknoe,* or an Oxford degree ceremony, as in *The Dunciad,* of the ascension of Christ at the end of *Erewhon,* a pattern which is the basis of a good deal of the satire in *Erewhon Revisited,* as well. It may be a historical event, or a series of events, like George Orwell's *Animal Farm* and

[10] Some of the traits of Gatsby's character, and some of the incidents of the opening chapters, are also patterned on the character of Trimalchio and the description of his dinner in Petronius' *The Satyricon.*

many other allegorical satires. It may be based upon biography, like some of the portraits in *Point Counter Point*, some of Peacock's and Waugh's novels, or in fact any *roman à clef* satire. Or, of course, it may be a combination of historical event and biography. Some satires of this kind are partly lampoons, and in many ONE of the purposes of the satire may be to lampoon an original. But this isn't necessarily the case. James Thurber's fine satiric short story *The Greatest Man in the World* is an account of Pal Smurch, an around-the-world flier who is everything a national hero ought not to be. Thurber has patterned Pal Smurch's exploit upon Charles Lindbergh's famous flight to Paris, but his main target is not Lindbergh. The recollection of the Lindbergh flight, and the impeccable reputation of its hero, give the reader a perspective from which to view the American demand for a faultless hero – and this demand is the primary object of Thurber's satire.

In one of the sketches in *Life with Father* Clarence Day tells the story of how difficult he found it to act naturally while wearing a pair of Father's Sunday trousers which had been handed down to him. The trousers retained something of the spirit of their original owner and seemed to insinuate a comment about the activities of their present occupant. Satiric patterns are like that: they not only provide a form, they imply a criticism. If Father's trousers had been passed on to someone who knew little or nothing of the original owner, their power of suggestion would have been lost. Similarly, a satiric pattern is most effective when the reader of the satire can recognize and respond to the insinuation of the pattern. For this reason most patterns seem to have been adopted while they were popular for non-satiric purposes, or at least easily recognizable, and abandoned when their suggestiveness faded.[11]

---

[11] For this reason minor satiric genres appear and disappear frequently. Pope's *A Receit To Make an Epick Poem* belongs to a minor genre which adopts its structure and some of its language from the cookery recipe. During the Restoration a series of satiric poems appeared whose pattern was imitated from Waller's *Instructions to a Painter* ... designed to *praise* the Duke of York for his victory over the Dutch fleet. The disasters to the English which shortly followed inspired a series of "Directions" poems which used the same general pattern for satiric purposes. During the late seventeenth and early eighteenth century a number of "Progress Pieces" were written. The basic plan was an allegory of the birth of an abstraction like Beauty, Wit, Patriotism, in one country and its "progress" to another. Sir John Denham's *Progress of Learning* (about 1669), and Lord Lansdowne's *Progress of Beauty* (1701) were followed by many others – including a number of satiric adaptations of the form. Swift's three "progress" poems, *The Progress of Beauty, The Progress of Poetry*, and *The Progress of Marriage*, and Pope's *The Dunciad*, which was originally entitled "The Progress of Dulness", are examples. See Mary Claire Randolph, "The Sinful Suburbs of Cookery: Satirical Recipes of the XVIIIth Century", *Notes and Queries*, CLXXXVI (1944), 32-36; Reginald

Thus mock-heroic satires were popular during the late seventeenth and early eighteenth centuries when the long popularity of the heroic poem, the constant discussion of its characteristics, the stylization of many of its features, the elevation of language, character and incident, made it a wonderfully effective vehicle for satiric matter. In a non-heroic age, the contrast between container and contents was easy to enforce. But it is not surprising that the popularity of the mock-heroic waned as interest in the epic declined.

The long popularity and widespread use of the heroic pattern is exceptional, however. The patterns many satirists have adapted are so ephemeral that the uninitiated reader may misinterpret a satire, or even be unaware that he is reading one if he does not recognize a pattern and the meaning it is intended to carry. It seems likely that when a detailed history of satiric patterns is written it will be at least as useful to the critic of the proteus of literary genres as to the literary historian.

Harvey Griffith, "The Progress Pieces of the Eighteenth Century", *The Texas Review*, V (1920), 218-233; Robert A. Aubin, "A Note on the Eighteenth Century Progress Pieces", *Modern Language Notes*, XLIX (1934), 405-407; and Mattie Swayne, "The Progress Piece in the Seventeenth Century", *University of Texas Bulletin: Studies in English*, No. 16 (1936), 84-92.

V

THE SPEAKERS IN SATIRE

The art of satire has long been recognized as essentially a rhetorical art, and the tactics of the satirist are regarded, to a large extent, as rhetorical, ordered to insinuate blame. A good part of the art of a rhetorician rests upon his skill in establishing the character of a speaker (usually identified as the rhetorician himself) who will appeal to his audience in ways which help to convince it of the soundness of his argument. Hardly surprising then is the fact that the satirist often finds it useful to embody a point of view in a speaker whose words, actions, or attitudes will help define the object of the satire and determine the feelings of the audience of the satire toward the object.

The kinds of speaker the satirist creates, the relationship of the speaker to the writer's own personality and attitudes, the effects of the speaker upon the total meaning of a given satire – none of these are new subjects, but they have been discussed with increasing frequency during the past fifteen or twenty years. Part of this attention is the result of a revival of interest in satire generally. Part, too, is the result of our growing awareness that if we are to understand the art of satire we must carefully distinguish between the writer of the satire and the speakers he has created as part of his satiric fiction. We are no longer willing to accept the common nineteenth century idea that Jonathan Swift was necessarily a misanthrope because Gulliver becomes one in the last book of *Gulliver's Travels*. We have become more aware of the consummate mastery of rhetoric which Alexander Pope displays in his Horatian Epistles and *Imitations of Horace*.

In the pages which follow I shall not try to cite and summarize all that recent critics have said about the various speakers satirists have used, nor shall I attempt to establish a series of watertight categories into which the characters of the satiric dramas may be filed. Satire is far too protean for any such tidy schematization. However, it will be useful to point out some of the ways in which the personalities of the writers of satire themselves, the characters they have created and, perhaps most important, the inextricable interpenetration of the two, contribute to the insinuation which is the manner of proceeding in any satire.

Whether or not it is possible to produce absolutely impersonal art is, I take it, hardly a serious critical question by now. Most of us would agree that no work of art is absolutely "scientific" or truly impersonal. In the work of even the most impenetrably reticent of writers we can discern attitudes toward certain things which are clearly the result of a human being's ideas about, or feelings toward, the subject. The drama is more impersonal than any other literary form; the author "says" nothing, the characters everything. Shakespeare is as apparently aloof, his personality apparently as elusive, as that of any English writer. Yet it is difficult to read even Shakespeare without concluding that we know something about the creator of the plays, his feelings about certain broad general subjects that vitally affect us all.

Our feeling that the author is not a detached observer is of course strong in satire since the essence of satire is to insinuate judgments, to imply blameworthy attitudes. The more we are aware of insinuation – or, in other words, the more we are aware that satiric tactics are being used – the more unmistakable our feeling that we are in the presence of satire. (This is true, I think, whether or not we can define the object of the satire with any precision, whether or not we can state the "norm" or "ideal" theoretically embodied in the satire. Our mere awareness that insinuating tactics are in play is sufficient.) These tactics are obviously being employed by someone to "get at" something else, and a person, the writer of the satire, is responsible for them. Satire is the least impersonal of literary forms.

Still, there are degrees to which the writer of the satire reveals himself. In some satires, particularly modern ones in the forms of novels or short stories, the writer of satire does not appear in his own person at all. In Ronald Firbank's novels, in most of Aldous Huxley's, in Herman Melville's *The Confidence Man* and in Terry Southern's *The Magic Christian,* insofar as we are aware of the personality or attitudes of the writer, we are aware because he has used certain tactics in such and such a way, because he has created certain characters and because he has chosen to attack certain things. All the tactics, working together, create what we might call a satiric tone. The creator of the tone, the satiric tactician, is a presence whom we respond to even though he does not speak to us directly.

The writer may be less reticent than this of course. Sometimes a voice we take to be the satirist's own cuts through the network of insinuation with a direct comment. When, in *Mac Flecknoe,* the narrator says Flecknoe was "own'd, without dispute,/ Thro' all the realms of *Nonsense,* absolute" (11. 5-6) we can hardly doubt that the flat word *"Nonsense"* is Dryden's voice speaking to us directly. We can hear the voice of Evelyn Waugh in the following passage of *The Loved One,* too. Dennis Barlow has come to Whispering Glades, which is to be the last resting place of his friend Sir Francis Hinsley, and is looking into the coffin:

The body looked altogether smaller than life-size now that it was, as it were, stripped of the thick pelt of mobility and intelligence. And the face which inclined its blind eyes towards him – the face was entirely horrible; as ageless as a tortoise and as inhuman; a painted and smirking obscene travesty by comparison with which the devil-mask Dennis had found in the noose was a festive adornment, a thing an uncle might don at a Christmas party.

(p. 61)

For a moment the tone of the satire changes. The narrator's bland, understated narration is interrupted; the veil of insinuation drops; and Waugh's own emotional reaction to the scene he is describing is apparent in "the face was entirely horrible . . . a painted and smirking obscene travesty . . .". For the moment Waugh has abandoned insinuation for emotion-charged direct statement.

Though each of the passages above occurs in a context of insinuating tactics, both are direct; we are expected to take what the author of the satire says at face value. Shifts like these are characteristic of mixed satires like *Mac Flecknoe.* In indirect satire they are sometimes the result of artistic flaws; the writer of the satire has for the moment lost control of his material. However, they may also be deliberately introduced to contrast with insinuation and thus lend it a sharper cutting edge, or to make sure that an important point, or points, cannot be overlooked or slighted.

Even though the writer of the satire does not confine himself to unequivocal statement, we need not assume that when he insinuates we must consider him an entirely different person. When the narrator of *The Dunciad* tells Jonathan Swift "Mourn not, my SWIFT, at aught our Realm acquires./ Here pleas'd behold her mighty wings out-spread/ To hatch a new Saturnian age of Lead." (V, 271, 11. 26-28; "Her" of course refers to the Goddess who reigns over Dulness), we need not

suppose that anyone but Alexander Pope is speaking. He doesn't literally mean that Swift should not "mourn", nor that Swift will be pleased
at the progress of Dulness, but the irony is clearly Pope's and not that
of some fictitious character. Charles Churchill's *Dedication to the
Sermons* begins:

> Health to great GLOSTER – from a man unknown,
> Who holds thy health as dearly as his own,
> Accept this greeting – nor let modest fear
> Call up one maiden blush – I mean not here
> To wound with flatt'ry – 'tis a Villain's art,
> And suits not with the frankness of my heart.
> Truth best becomes an *Orthodox* Divine,
> And, spite of hell, that Character is mine;
> To speak e'en bitter truths I cannot fear;
> But truth, *my Lord,* is panegyric here.[1]

There is no doubt that, despite the insinuation, Churchill here is speaking in his own person. The references to himself not only in the lines
above but elsewhere in the poem make this clear. Churchill does not
mean us to take what he says literally any more than Pope does, but
he works more subtly. The mock-heroic opening of *The Dunciad* gives
us a clear line on how to read Pope's words to Swift, but there is no
such clear indication here. The poem begins as a panegyric and the
speaker embarks upon a flight of the most fulsome praise. Or apparently
embarks, for we gradually begin to realize that the panegyric is insulting
– that the praise is actually a skillful and savage indictment of the
Bishop of Gloster.

In all the mixed or indirect satires I have just mentioned, though
the writer of the satire speaks he remains merely a voice. There are
some touches of characterization in the *Dedication,* but they hardly
flesh out a personality. The personality of the writer of the satire may
of course play a much larger role, one in which the picture of himself
which he chooses to present to his audience is a most important satiric
tactic. Dr. Johnson's famous letter to Lord Chesterfield is such a perfect
example that it is worth quoting in full:

'MY LORD,
    'I have been lately informed, by the proprietor of *The World,* that two
papers, in which my Dictionary is recommended to the publick, were
written by your Lordship. To be so distinguished, is an honour, which,
being very little accustomed to favours from the great, I know not well
how to receive, or in what terms to acknowledge.

---

[1] *The Poetical Works of Charles Churchill*, ed. Douglas Grant (Oxford, 1956),
p. 431.

'When, upon some slight encouragement, I first visited your Lordship, I was overpowered, like the rest of mankind, by the enchantment of your address; and could not forbear to wish that I might boast myself *Le vainqueur du vainqueur de la terre*; – that I might obtain that regard for which I saw the world contending; but I found my attendance so little encouraged, that neither pride nor modesty would suffer me to continue it. When I had once addressed your Lordship in publick, I had exhausted all the art of pleasing which a retired and uncourtly scholar can possess. I had done all that I could; and no man is well pleased to have his all neglected, be it ever so little.

'Seven years, my Lord, have now past, since I waited in your outward rooms, or was repulsed from your door; during which time I have been pushing on my work through difficulties, of which it is useless to complain, and have brought it, at last, to the verge of publication, without one act of assistance, one word of encouragement, or one smile of favour. Such treatment I did not expect, for I never had a Patron before.

'The shepherd in Virgil grew at last acquainted with Love, and found him a native of the rocks.

'Is not a Patron, my Lord, one who looks with unconcern on a man struggling for life in the water, and, when he has reached ground, encumbers him with help? The notice which you have been pleased to take of my labours, had it been early, had been kind; but it has been delayed till I am indifferent, and cannot enjoy it; till I am solitary, and cannot impart it; till I am known, and do not want it. I hope it is no very cynical asperity not to confess obligations where no benefit has been received, or to be unwilling that the Publick should consider me as owing that to a Patron, which Providence has enabled me to do for myself.

'Having carried on my work thus far with so little obligation to any favourer of learning, I shall not be disappointed though I should conclude it, if less be possible, with less; for I have been long wakened from that dream of hope, in which I once boasted myself with so much exultation, my Lord, your Lordship's most humble, most obedient servant,

'Sam Johnson'[2]

Johnson's picture of himself as a "retired and uncourtly scholar", repulsed by a noble man of the world, left to struggle in obscurity until his work is completed and proudly rejecting support he no longer needed, doubtless is an accurate enough portrait in general outline. But it has been finely shaped by a satiric rhetorician who continually keeps us aware of the contrast between the humble, but proud, deserving scholar and the glittering but shallow aristocrat – and in this carefully shaped antithesis lies the essence of the satiric thrust, not only at Chesterfield, but at the whole decaying system of aristocratic patronage of the arts.

Though there are some touches of insinuation, Johnson's letter

---

[2] *Boswell's Life of Johnson* (Oxford, 1948), I, 173-175.

belongs to direct satire. E. B. White's letter to the Collector of Internal Revenue creates a satiric antithesis, too, but the thrust is much less overt. The letter is a reply to an official notice that a warrant has been issued for the "seizure and sale" of White's place in Maine for failure to pay income taxes. The open letter in reply is a delightfully rambling, whimsical account of White's troubles with the Society for the Prevention of Cruelty to Animals which has accused him of "harboring an unleashed dog" in his New York apartment, of his dogs and the house he has built for them, of a goose which is setting on eggs in his barn, and a good deal else. It ends:

I am sore about your note, which didn't seem friendly. I am a friendly taxpayer and do not think the government should take a threatening tone, at least until we have exchanged a couple of letters kicking the thing around. Then it might be all right to talk about selling the place, if I proved stubborn. I showed the lawyer your notice about the warrant of seizure and sale, and do you know what he said? He said, "Oh, that doesn't mean anything, it's just a form." What a crazy way to look at a piece of plain English. I honestly worry about lawyers. They never write plain English themselves, and when you give them a bit of plain English to read, they say, "Don't worry, it doesn't mean anything." They're hopeless, don't you think they are? To me a word is a word, and I wouldn't dream of writing anything like "I am going to get out a warrant to seize and sell your place" unless I meant it, and I can't believe that my government would either.

The best way to get into the house is through the woodshed, as there is an old crocus sack nailed on the bottom step and you can wipe the mud off on it. Also, when you go in through the woodshed, you land in the back kitchen right next to the cooky jar with Mrs. Freethy's cookies. Help yourself, they're wonderful.

Sincerely yours,
E. B. White[3]

White's apparently ingenuous account of himself and his household embodies a couple of nice satiric points. The first is a thrust at the apersonal jargon of bureaucracy. His own informal, personal style is an implicit commentary upon it. The other is a dig at bureaucracy itself, to which White's own fumbling, inefficient, but warmly human personality is the perfect satiric foil.

The portraits of themselves which Johnson and White present to their readers are rhetorically ordered, but nonetheless seem reasonably accurate. Shaped, certainly, but recognizable. The process of shaping is carried a good deal further in some satires. The writer of the satire

---

[3] "Two Letters, Both Open", in *The Second Tree from the Corner* (New York, 1954), pp. 87-88.

may present himself as a simpleton or ingénu. Thus the speaker in
"The General Prologue" to *The Canterbury Tales* listens to the Monk's
argument for the active, worldly life and blandly agrees " I seyde his
opinion was good."[4] Alexander Pope, James Thurber and Mark Twain
all present themselves at times as artless innocents, too simple to understand the iniquity of the situations in which they are involved. Charles
Churchill, part of whose *Dedication* I quoted above, represents himself
as an innocent, also. A profession of innocence is often accompanied
by, in fact frequently inseparable from, wry self-depreciation of the
sort Chaucer is fond of and which we often notice in satires by James
Thurber, Mark Twain, E. B. White, and even Alexander Pope. Assuming the role of innocence and of self-depreciation is not to be taken too
seriously of course. The writer of the satire is playing a role, one which
is closely related to his own personality but which has been artfully
contrived to focus, or to further, the point of the satire. Though the
writer, as ingénu, professes not to understand the implications of the
situations in which he finds himself, our recognition that there is a gap
between what he sees and what we do is an important part of the satiric
effect. The writer who depreciates himself may be pointing up the
arrogance or pride of others by his own humility, or winning sympathy
which will be denied to those who oppose or abuse him. Whatever the
case, the writer of the satire uses the role he plays as one of the tactics
in the satire.

In the examples I have cited above there has been evident, I trust,
a kind of progression from rhetorical uses of the speaker in satire in
which the portrait is close to what we assume is the writer's "real"
personality, to those in which the element of artifice seems more and
more obvious. From this point it is only a step to the creation of figures
who are quite distinct from the writer of the satire, even though they
speak in the first person. "Impersonations" like this were part of the
standard training in the Greek and Roman rhetorical schools and in
one form or another have always been one of the most important tactics
in satire.

A satiric character like this is often called a "persona" after the Latin
word *persona*, meaning not only "person", but "mask" or "character"
as well. The term has gained a good deal of currency in recent criticism

---

[4] Two useful, though conflicting, discussions of the "I" of the "Prologue" are
E. Talbot Donaldson, "Chaucer the Pilgrim", *PMLA*, LXIX (1954), 928-936, and
John M. Major, "The Personality of Chaucer the Pilgrim", *PMLA*, LXXV (1960),
160-162.

and is usually applied, to quote a current handbook of literary terms, "to what has often been called the *voice* (or *mask)* speaking in any work. The speaker is not the author, but the author's creation."[5] For our purposes we should limit this definition a little. A persona in satire is a created character whom we must clearly differentiate from the literal, historical person of the writer of the satire, though he speaks in the first person. What he says or does not say, may reflect adversely upon himself and, to the extent that it does, the persona may be the object or one of the objects of the satire. In *Holy Willie's Prayer,* for example, the speaker is Willie himself, and a part of the satire is at his expense. More typically, however, the words of the speaker are chiefly intended to be a medium of insinuating blame about someone, or something, else. The prime object of the satire in *A Modest Proposal* is not the speaker himself, but, to put it as briefly as possible, everyone and everything responsible for the conditions that exist in contemporary Ireland.

The persona often delivers a monologue; all that we learn about him and what he represents is embodied in his own words. In some satiric works we can see him struggling as it were to emerge from passages of third-person description. Earlier, I quoted passages from Chaucer's satiric portraits of the Friar and the Monk in which for a few lines the object of the satire speaks for himself. Another embryonic persona seems to be struggling to emerge from the elder Samuel Butler's Character, *A Modern Politician.* Most seventeenth century Characters are written in the third person. If the Character is satiric, as many are, we see the object of the satire only from the outside. Most of what we learn about *A Modern Politician* is from the exterior, but in one section we can hear a persona struggling to voice his own opinions. The Character is a long one; during most of it Butler describes the politician in rather general terms. But about halfway through, the following passage occurs:

Next Pride he believes Ambition to be the only generous and heroical Virtue in the World, that Mankind is capable of. For as Nature gave Man an erect Figure, to raise him above the groveling Condition of his fellow Creatures the Beasts: so he, that endeavours to improve that, and raise himself higher, seems best to comply with the Design and Intention of Nature. Though the Stature of Man is confined to a certain Height, yet his Mind is unlimited, and capable of growing up to Heaven: And as those, who endeavour to arrive at that Perfection, are adored and reverenced by all; so he, that endeavours to advance himself as high as possibly he can

[5] Sylvan Barnet, Morton Berman, William Burto, *A Dictionary of Literary Terms* (Boston and Toronto, 1960), p. 66.

in this World, comes nearest to the Condition of those holy and divine Aspiers. All the purest Parts of Nature always tend upwards, and the more dull and heavy downwards: so in the little World the noblest Faculties of Man, his Reason and Understanding, that give him a Prerogative above all other earthly Creatures, mount upwards – And therefore he, who takes that Course and still aspires in all his Undertakings and Designs, does but conform to that which Nature dictates – Are not the Reason and the Will, the two commanding Faculties of the Soul, still striving which shall be uppermost? Men honour none but those that are above them, contest with Equals, and disdain Inferiors. The first Thing that God gave Man, was Dominion over the rest of his inferior Creatures; but he, that can extend that over Man, improves his Talent to the best Advantage.[6]

Description gives way to dramatization. For a moment the type comes alive. He is justifying himself. We have, not a description, but a glimpse into the mind of the man himself; for a moment Character almost becomes persona.

John Oldham's *Satires upon the Jesuits* carries the process a step further. There are several personas in the poem. The one who opens it is the familiar speaker of formal verse satire. He rains direct abuse upon the Jesuits. But the other personas are identified as the Jesuits Garnet and Loyola. What they say reflects discredit not upon something else, but upon themselves and their order. Here we have crudely but unmistakably the persona of indirect satire.

In each of the cases mentioned above, the words of the personas are part of a larger structure. Blame is insinuated partly as a result of what the persona says himself, but partly as a result of what we learn from other sources. In purest form, the persona of indirect satire is revealed entirely through his own words. Sometimes we merely over-hear him thinking or praying; sometimes he is addressing a person or a group; sometimes he has a plan or project to present, or a narrative to tell. But whatever he says, whatever his ostensible reason for speaking, the effect of what the persona says is not the one he intends.

There are various ways in which the persona is used. In *The Shortest Way with the Dissenters* Defoe attacks the High-flying Tories by cre-ating a persona who states their position so violently that the reader is impelled to condemn them instead of the Dissenters. Swift works more subtly in *An Argument Against Abolishing Christianity*. His

---

[6] *Characters and Passages from Note-Books*, ed. A. R. Waller (Cambridge, 1908), pp. 7-8. I owe the point discussed above to Ricardo Quintana, "Samuel Butler: A Restoration Figure in a Modern Light", *ELH, A Journal of English Literary History*, XVIII (1951), 30.

object was to attack those who preserved the outer forms of Christianity without its real substance. One way of doing this would have been to have a persona argue FOR the abolition of Christianity. His persona[7] is one of the hypocritical Christians, but instead of arguing that Christianity should be abolished, he argues that it should be retained and lists a variety of reasons for its retention. The reasons are discreditable ones which the reader rejects, but in the course of rejecting them, the reader sees clearly the state of contemporary Christianity as Swift wants him to see it.

The personas of satire are a varied lot, since the type of persona varies with satirist and object. They tend to fall into two general groups, however. The first of these is the group to which belong the personas of Defoe and Swift that I have just mentioned. This persona is relatively aggressive. He is usually sure of himself; often he is objectionably cocksure. He is fond of superlatives. The "best", the "worst", the "least", the "most" are staples of his vocabulary.[8] He is certain of his own rectitude, or that of the country, group, or profession he represents. However, though sure of his own rightness, he may declare that the world has wronged him, or that he deserves a better place than the one fortune or the times have allowed him. Sometimes he has a plan or project which will right a wrong, alleviate distress, or enable the deserving young to progress in the world. He may take it upon himself to espouse a cause, or to defend one with which he is associated. But whatever he says, the effect is not the one he ostensibly intends. His words make it clear to the reader that he himself is lacking in wisdom or moral sense, but these are incidental effects. The primary effect is to make the reader aware, through the agency of the persona, that a blameworthy situation exists which the persona sees differently than does the reader. His words reveal a world which has only a single focus for him, but more than one for us. We see the world not only as he does, but as the writer of the satire wants us to see it. This second

---

[7] Swift's use of the persona has been discussed in detail in William Bragg Ewald Jr., *The Masks of Jonathan Swift* (Cambridge, Massachusetts, 1954).
[8] The projector of *A Modest Proposal* hopes that his proposal "will not be liable to the least Objection". (Swift, *Prose Works*, XII [1955], 111.) Pope's persona in *A Receit To Make an Epick Poem* says "that kind of Literature ... at present carried on ... consists *only* in a Knowledge of Mechanick Rules ..." (*Prose Works*, p. 115. The italics are mine.) The effect of course is to raise the reader's hackles – to set him searching for exceptions to the rule so forcefully laid down, and thus to cooperate, wittingly or unwittingly, with the writer of the satire.

focus is the one which reveals the meaning of the satire, and in our act of shifting lies the essence of the satiric effect.[9]

The second common type of persona is an ingénu. He is an innocent, a lamentably naive person who doesn't really understand the situations into which he is thrust or in which he finds himself. Sometimes he simply describes a situation he himself does not understand. At times he makes no comment at all; at others he misses the implication or point; frequently he praises when the reader knows he should be blaming. The kind, and degree, of the ingénu's lack of comprehension varies from a mild, hardly culpable one to perverse moral blindness, but whatever the case the gap between what he understands and what the writer of the satire insinuates the reader should understand is crucial.

How much we learn about the individual persona varies greatly. We always learn something about the way his mind, and those of people like him, operate, but sometimes little more. In *The Shortest Way with the Dissenters,* we learn little about the speaker and this has to be inferred from what he says about the Dissenters. Other personas reveal themselves much more fully. We know a good deal about the projector in *A Modest Proposal,* about Holy Willie, Gulliver, and the narrator of *Erewhon.*

The details we learn contribute to the verisimilitude of the portrait and help distinguish the point of view of the author from that of the persona. Usually they are intended to do more than merely round out a character, however; they contribute to the tone of the satire, or help make a satiric point. When the projector of *A Modest Proposal* tells us: "I have no Children, by which I can propose to get a single Penny; the youngest being nine Years old, and my Wife past Child-bearing"[10] the domestic details are in themselves less important than what they contribute to the tone of dispassionate impartiality with which the projector speaks. Similarly, the early adventures of the narrator in *Erewhon,* his attempt to convert Chowbok, for example, are not only interesting in their own right, but contribute to making the narrator's self-seeking evangelism seem real, and to making a point about the motives and ethics of "Christian" exploitation of native peoples.

But details individualize, and individualizing may be carried too far. The persona is intended to suggest a viewpoint for viewing a situation.

[9] The role of the persona is similar in a number of ways to that of the speaker of the dramatic monologue. For an illuminating discussion of the latter see Robert Langbaum, *The Poetry of Experience* (New York, 1963), esp. p. 146.
[10] Swift, *Prose Works,* XII (1955), 118.

A portrait which emphasizes the peculiarities of the persona is likely to draw attention to him, rather than to the satiric point to which he is intended to guide the reader. The most distinctive types of persona do not develop or change, for they are usually intended to focus insinuation upon a single satiric point, or at least a group of closely associated ones. A persona who develops or changes moves closer to the more rounded, complex characters found in non-satiric works; hence any satire in which a developing persona is used is likely to be close to the borders of satire. Satires in which proper personas are used tend to be short and, if they are in prose, based upon essay or short-story patterns. In William Faulkner's *Spotted Horses,* Ring Lardner's *Haircut,* and George Milburn's *The Apostate,* for example, the personas narrate short-stories. Longer satiric works in which a persona is used are likely to be episodic, and the persona may shift his ground or develop to the point at which he can scarcely be said to be a persona at all. I shall want to discuss the personas of longer satires like *Erewhon* and *Gulliver's Travels* in some detail a little later.

Some personas are real persons, and are identified as such: *Hudibras* Butler's "John Audland" and "William Prynne", Swift's "Thomas Wharton", and Burns' "Holy Willie", for example. Others, like the persona of Swift's *A Discourse To Prove the Antiquity of the English Tongue,* who seems to be based on Richard Bentley, suggest that a real person's style or methods were at least the point of departure, though the actual subject of the parody may not be named. Quite frequently the language the persona uses, or the methods he adopts, suggest parody, even though the original cannot be identified.

One type of aggressive persona which occurs time and again might be called the Ingenious Critic. He is usually a literary critic who sees implications or tendencies which others have missed. Pope employed him a number of times. In *A Clue to the Comedy of the Non-Juror* the Ingenious Critic sees all sorts of political and religious meanings in Colley Cibber's adaptation of Molière's *Tartuffe,* and in *A Key to the Lock* and *A Master Key to Popery* he examines with a keen eye the work of Pope himself. The former is a light, amusing piece in which the "author," one Esdras Barnivelt, examines *The Rape of the Lock* in some detail and concludes that it is both a "Satyr" upon the signing of the Barrier Treaty, and "has a tendency to Popery, which is secretly insinuated through the whole".[11] *A Master Key to Popery* has a more serious tone. The persona is concerned to show the "Bad Heart" of

[11] Pope, *Prose Works,* p. 197.

Pope, who, he avers, has attacked contemporary architecture and those responsible for it in the *Epistle* to the Earl of Burlington. The persona misquotes, insists upon making specific applications where (Pope insinuates) general ones were intended, allows that Pope has "some Genius" and insists that it is *"Only his Morals"* [12] that he attacks, though he is plainly wrong-headed. In short, he exhibits the characteristics of a *bad* critic.

Swift puts the Ingenious Critic to various tasks. In *A Discourse To Prove the Antiquity of the English Tongue* he "proves" that the English language was originally "the same with those of the Jews, the Greeks, and the Romans, however corrupted in succeeding times by a mixture of barbarisms". In Latin, for example, the "word *Turpis* signifieth *nasty,* or *filthy.* Now this word *Turpis* is a plain composition of two English words; only by a syncope, the last letter of the first syllable, which is *d*, is taken out of the middle, to prevent the jarring of three consonants together: And these two English words express the two most unseemly excrements that belong to man." [13] In the 22nd number of *The Examiner* Swift assumes the mask of one of the opposition faction and examines one of his own papers.

The personas of Pope's *A Receit To Make an Epick Poem* and Swift's *A Letter of Advice to a Young Poet* are Ingenious Critics as well, but they survey wider fields than most of their fellows. Each has studied literature and arrived at certain conclusions which are passed on to aspiring writers. Their conclusions, of course, are unsound. What their advice amounts to is how to write a bad epic, and how to write trashy poetry. Frederick C. Crews and Ronald Knox have given us a number of more recent versions of the Ingenious Critic. Crews' *The Pooh Perplex* contains a whole series of "explications" of the Winnie the Pooh books done by different practicioners of the most approved modern critical methods. Knox's *Essays in Satire* contains several fine incarnations of the same genus. In "The Authorship of 'In Memoriam' " the critic uses the anagrammatic and cryptographic methods devised by Shakespearean critics and comes to the conclusion that "In Memoriam", though published under Tennyson's name, was written by Queen Victoria as a memorial to Lord Melbourne. In "The Identity of the Pseudo-Bunyan" the conclusions are even more dramatic. The critic applies modern methods of Biblical criticism to John Bunyan's work and concludes after a careful sifting of the evidence that Part II of *Pilgrim's*

---

[12]   *Poems*, 2nd ed., III ii, p. 177.
[13]   Swift, *Prose Works*, IV (1957), 232.

Progress was written "by an Anglican with tendencies in the Catholic direction, perhaps one who only waited for the Duke of York's accession to come out as a supporter of the Old Religion. . . ."[14] Moreover, the evidence points to the conclusion that the author was "a woman, jealous for the credit of her own sex. . . ."[15]

There is a good deal of pure fun in Knox's satire, as there is in much of Augustan satire, but his persona's application of critical methods, and the conclusions that result make his point about "modern" exegesis of the Bible more deftly than any amount of direct denunciation could.

Some Ingenious Critics are not meant to be identified with specific individuals, others are. Yet even when the satire is partly personal, the attack includes other critics with the same tendencies. The assault is an oblique one. There are sound methods of criticism, and sound critics – but this criticism and these critics are not among them.

The ingénu is sometimes the central figure in a traveller's tale. He reports what he sees, comments occasionally, but lets the incidents he describes carry the main burden of the satire. In one of Goldsmith's *Citizen of the World* letters, Lien Chi Altangi reports a conversation among an imprisoned debtor, a porter who has stopped to rest his burden, and a soldier. The prisoner fears an invasion from France; the liberty of Englishmen will be in danger. The porter is contemptuous of Frenchmen: "they are all slaves, fit only to carry burthens. . . ." The soldier's main fear is that English religion will suffer: "*May the devil sink me into flames . . . if the French should come over, but our religion would be utterly undone.*"[16] Lien Chi Altangi passes on to another topic without comment.

The ingénu is familiar in comic as well as in satiric writing. In comic works which contain satiric elements, the ingénu serves the same purpose as he does in indirect satire proper. James Thurber and Mark Twain, as I have mentioned, often pose as ingénus and Huck, in *Huckleberry Finn*, despite strong individualizing features, often functions in much the same way as does the speaker in "The General Prologue" to *The Canterbury Tales*. Characters like Paul Pennyfeather and Adam Fenwick-Symes in Evelyn Waugh's *Decline and Fall* and *Vile Bodies*, and John the Savage in Aldous Huxley's *Brave New*

---

[14] Knox, *Essays in Satire* (London, 1928), p. 218.
[15] Knox, *Essays in Satire*, p. 219.
[16] Letter IV, in *Goldsmith: Selected Works*, ed. Richard Garnett (London, 1950), p. 290.

World – though they are not personas in the narrowest sense – often point up an insinuation. Paul, for example, has been sent to prison for a crime committed by his bride-to-be, Margot Beste-Chetwynde.

He had "done the right thing" in shielding the woman: so much was clear, but Margot had not quite filled the place assigned to her, for in this case she was grossly culpable, and he was shielding her, not from misfortune nor injustice, but from the consequence of her crimes; . . . he had wrestled with this argument without achieving any satisfactory result except a growing conviction that there was something radically inapplicable about this whole code of ready-made honour that is the still small voice, trained to command, of the Englishman all the world over. On the other hand was the undeniable cogency of Peter Beste-Chetwynde's "You can't see Mamma in prison, can you?" The more Paul considered this, the more he perceived it to be the statement of a natural law. He appreciated the assumption of comprehension with which Peter had delivered it. As he studied Margot's photograph . . . he was strengthened in his belief that there was, in fact, and should be, one law for her and another for himself, and that the raw little exertions of nineteenth-century Radicals were essentially base and trivial and misdirected.[17]

As I suggested above, most of the satires in which a full-fledged persona is used are relatively short. If a persona is used in a longer satire, he is likely to shift roles as Mr. Higgs does in *Erewhon*. *Erewhon* is episodic, a series of satiric essays connected by a thread of narrative and by the commentary of Mr. Higgs, the narrator. The essays are enveloped by the introductory and concluding chapters which bring Higgs to *Erewhon,* take him away from it, and reveal his plan for "Christianizing" the country. In these envelope chapters, Higgs is clearly an aggressive persona with a project. He early hints at great schemes, and in the concluding chapters outlines the project by which "I will guarantee that I convert the Erewhonians not only into good Christians but into a source of considerable profit to the shareholders" (p. 305).[18] The plan is to invade Erewhon with an armed force, take large numbers of Erewhonians to Queensland by persuasion or force and sell them into the service of the sugar-growers. The money thus realized would pay handsome profits to the sponsors of the scheme, and "benefit" the Erewhonians themselves, for they would be

[17]   Evelyn Waugh, *Decline and Fall* (Harmondsworth, Middlesex, 1951), pp. 187-188.
[18]   Samuel Butler, *Erewhon and Erewhon Revisited*, Modern Library (New York, 1927).

boarded and lodged in the households of religious sugargrowers; these persons would give them the benefit of that instruction whereof they stand so greatly in need. Each day, as soon as they could be spared from their work in the plantations, they would be assembled for praise, and be thoroughly grounded in the Church Catechism, while the whole of every Sabbath should be devoted to singing psalms and church-going.

(p. 304)

Here, clearly, is the voice of the aggressive persona.

Higgs also assumes the role of the ingénu. When he describes the customs which accompany the birth and coming of age of an Erewhonian child, customs which bear a more than fortuitous relationship to the Christian customs of baptism and confirmation, the parallel is apparently lost on him. The question he asks one of the Professors of Unreason is a loaded one.

I remember asking him whether he did not think it would do harm to a lad's principles, by weakening his sense of the sanctity of his word and of truth generally, that he should be led into entering upon a solemn declaration as to the truth of things about which all that he can certainly know is that he knows nothing – whether, in fact, the teachers who so led him, or who taught anything as a certainty of which they were themselves uncertain, were not earning their living by impairing the truth-sense of their pupils (a delicate organization mostly), and by vitiating one of their most sacred instincts.

(p. 178)

The answer he receives – that the "world was full of compromises" with truth, and that the customs were long-established – is as unsatisfactory as the answer to most ingénu's questions.

Perhaps it would be more accurate to say that Higgs POSES as an ingénu in the passage quoted above, for the mask is a thin one and direct criticism of the Erewhonian system is covered by the lightest of veils. The veil is completely off when Higgs discusses the relationships of parents and children. He says that he has observed only a few families in which "the children, even at the age of twenty, were fonder of their parents than they were of any one else" (p. 191) and reflects:

... I firmly believe that the same thing would happen in nine families out of ten if the parents were merely to remember how they felt when they were young, and actually to behave towards their children as they would have had their own parents behave towards themselves.

(p. 192)

The speaker here is neither an aggressive persona nor an ingénu whose apparent naïveté points up an insinuation which we will understand, even if he will not. This is simply a statement by Samuel Butler who is using Higgs as his mouthpiece.

The same sort of shifts occur in both of Swift's longer satires. The Grub Street hack of *A Tale of a Tub* shifts roles in a brilliant virtuoso performance which often leaves the reader agape in an effort to decide how to tune his ear to the tone of a given section, or even paragraph. In a famous paragraph of the climactic Section IX we have hardly adjusted our set to allow for the sophistry of the hack's argument that the appearances of things are preferable to a knowledge of their inner reality when an icy, quite different voice tells us directly: "This is the sublime and refined Point of Felicity, called, *the Possession of being well deceived;* The Serene Peaceful State of being a Fool among Knaves."[19]

Gulliver is hardly less complex. He is often called a persona, but changes roles too frequently and develops too much to be a persona in the restricted sense of the term. Sometimes he assumes the role of the aggressive persona, sometimes the ingénu, and sometimes he employs direct statement or conscious irony (on occasions like this he seems to be a mouthpiece for Swift himself).

The true persona is static; Gulliver learns and develops. Throughout Part I he learns the ways of princes and of courts, and finally says "I resolved never more to put any confidence in Princes or Ministers, where I could possibly avoid it." He ends his visit at the Court of Blefescu on a note of conscious irony: "I was resolved to venture myself in the Ocean, rather than be an Occasion of Difference between two such mighty Monarchs."[20]

Gulliver's development continues throughout the whole of *Gulliver's Travels*. He learns by studying Man, and by Part IV his education has reached the point that his revulsion from what Man is, or has become, is so complete that he longs for nothing more than to isolate himself from men, to live a life of cool, unimpassioned "Reason" among the Houyhnhnms.

During *Gulliver's Travels* the point of view varies as Gulliver's role as persona varies. In the first two parts Swift's point of view is relatively easy to separate from Gulliver's. In Part III, however, the irony which Gulliver sometimes employs is likely to suggest that Swift is merging HIS point of view with that of the persona, and in Part IV, where the satire reaches an unparalleled intensity the temptation to equate Swift

---

[19]   Swift, *Prose Works*, I (1957), 110.
[20]   Swift, *Prose Works*, XI (1959), 77.

and Gulliver has sometimes proved irresistible. But Gulliver, whose diatribe against Pride is the climax of Part IV, is clearly guilty of the sin of Pride himself. The effect is to indict not only others, but himself.

The satire goes deeper than this. Insofar as the reader himself accepts Gulliver's position, he, too, is involved in the satiric indictment, and is condemned. Usually the reader can keep himself separate from the objects of the satire he is reading. When he cannot – when he becomes so involved in the satiric work that the truth of the satire is proved upon his own pulses – satire perhaps can go no further.

The persona, as I have suggested, is a character created to act as a focus of, or medium for, insinuation, and is frequently found in satire proper, and often as well in mixed satire. Another sort of created character is most characteristic of direct satire, though he sometimes appears in the other channels, too. He is usually called simply the "Satirist", a somewhat unfortunate term since it is likely to suggest that he is to be identified with the literal, historical figure of the writer of the satire. In point of fact, like the persona, he is a character created to serve a rhetorical purpose though he, too, is sometimes confused with his creator.

The key difference between persona and Satirist is the difference between satire proper and direct satire. The persona insinuates; the Satirist attacks directly. I have already mentioned some of his characteristics in connection with Defoe's *The True-Born Englishman*, but it may be worth amplifying these remarks and making some distinctions before leaving the subject.

The Satirist[21] normally speaks directly to his audience, although occasionally he may speak to someone else within the satire, in which case his readers overhear a dialogue. He speaks directly to the point. Though he may occasionally use inversion, or some other form of irony, his normal mode of discourse is overstatement. He is usually a plain man who speaks without artifice, a simple man of humble, or at least undistinguished, background. The values he cherishes are the conservative ones of his forefathers. But though normally slow to take offense, he can be roused and, in the satire in which he speaks, has been roused by the follies and vices which thrust themselves upon him.

---

[21] The best description of the Satirist is found in Eugene M. Waith, *The Pattern of Tragicomedy in Beaumont and Fletcher*, Yale Studies in English, CXX (New Haven, 1952), Chapter II, and Alvin Kernan, *The Cankered Muse: Satire of the English Renaissance*, Yale Studies in English, CXLII (New Haven, 1959), Chapter I. In the account below I have followed the latter, pp. 14-30.

The world he sees is one in which, typically, the physical senses have mastered reason and overthrown the moral order. Though the Satirist cries out against the follies and vices of the world, he has little real hope that they will be mended. Often he pictures himself as the sole sane man left in a world overrun with unreason. In a situation like this, who can help writing satire?

But the Satirist, despite his pose of honest virtue, has another side. The violence of his language, his delight in portraying ordure and filth, his overweening egotism, all suggest chinks in his own armor. Occasionally he admits his faults openly. Alexander Pope, assuming the role of the Satirist in Dialogue II of the *Epilogue to the Satires,* admits himself guilty of a cardinal sin by Augustan standards: "Yes, I am proud; I must be proud to see/ Men not afraid of God, afraid of me."[22] The Satirist in one of George Wither's poems says:

> An Execut'oner am I,
> Of Lust, and wanton Venery.
> Thus are vices scourg'd by mee,
> Yet my selfe from vice not free;
> Like to Sumners that cite others,
> When themselves defile their mothers.[23]

Admission of faults like these of course serves a rhetorical purpose. It may establish that the speaker is a person who knows whereof he speaks, since who knows sin better than a deep-dyed sinner? It may help to establish the Satirist as a fallible human being, one who confesses to all-too-mortal failings of his own and pretends to no extraordinary virtue. Or it may help to demonstrate how corrupt and evil the times are. Everyone, including the Satirist, has been infected by the prevailing corruption.

Though he is a stock figure, the Satirist is sometimes easily confused with his creator; at times, in fact, he is hardly distinguishable from him. Pope frequently calls his Satirist "Alexander Pope" and it would be perverse to doubt that many of the views his Satirist expresses are indeed his own. But there is always an element of artifice. Pope is playing a role, or roles, as Maynard Mack has pointed out. Sometimes the role is that of the *"vir bonus*, the plain good private citizen", sometimes that of the "hero", or "public defender" who defends the public

---

[22]   *Poems*, 2nd ed., IV, 324, ll. 208-209.
[23]   George Wither, "Vices Executioner: or *The Satyr's selfe-description of himselfe*", quoted in Waith, *The Pattern of Tragicomedy*, p. 57.

weal.[24] These roles are both something more and something less than the character of the poet himself. In a phrase, they are rhetorically shaped figures designed to forward the purposes of the poems in which they occur. Doubtless they reflect the poet's own personality and views, but they are shaped to conform to the tradition of the Satirist who is a familiar figure not only in English Augustan and Renaissance satires, but in the classical originals upon which all are more or less closely modelled.

If we know something about the personality and opinions of the writer of the satire we can sometimes detect a divergence between his private views and those of his creation. Samuel Johnson's first formal verse satire, *London*, is a case in point. Many of the views the Satirist expresses can reasonably be attributed to Johnson himself. Others cannot. Joseph Wood Krutch remarks that some of the sentiments expressed in the poem are considerably in excess of what the facts seem to warrant, or are even contrary to what Johnson is known to have believed. He points out "the conventional contrast between the country and the city, which is little short of fantastic coming as it does from a man who was as completely and contentedly urban as any who ever lived."[25] Yet both the overstatement and preference for country over city life are venerable literary traditions, and perfectly consonant with the stock role of the Satirist. Johnson's opinions and those of his creation diverge, but the divergence is hardly an artistic flaw in the poem unless we insist upon identifying the two. In his second satire, *The Vanity of Human Wishes,* we are not conscious of any such divergence. The somber, declamatory voice of the Satirist in the poem is so typically Johnsonian, the views expressed so in consonance with those we attribute to Johnson himself, that it is difficult to mark any clear line of demarcation between Johnson and his Satirist. Yet the Satirists in both poems are both recognizable members of the group we have been discussing. The poet who has written *The Vanity of Human Wishes* has simply found in both subject and character a perfect role to play.

The Satirist appears most frequently and in his most familiar form in the formal verse satire of the sixteenth to eighteenth centuries. All of these bear, or at least were intended to bear, a fairly close resemblance to the satires of the Roman formal verse satirists. However,

[24] See "The Muse of Satire" in *Discussions of Alexander Pope*, edited with an Introduction by R. A. Blanshard (Boston, 1960), p. 104. Mack mentions a third role as well, that of the naïf or ingénu. The latter of course is typical of mixed, or indirect, satire.
[25] *Samuel Johnson* (New York, 1944), p. 63.

recognizable variations of the Satirist appear in all sorts of satiric verse, whether or not their authors have been influenced by classical satire – in Lollard anti-clerical satiric verse and the poems of John Skelton, in Byron's *English Bards and Scotch Reviewers* and in the free-swinging modern verse satires of our contemporary, Roy Campbell. They are found in different kinds of literary genres – in Ben Jonson's *Every Man out of his Humour,* and in some of the early novels of Tobias Smollett.[26] They appear in prose from medieval sermons to contemporary works like Philip Wylie's *Generation of Vipers* and the volcanic newspaper columns of Westbrook Pegler.

Though the Satirist is primarily a creature of direct satire, he may appear in mixed satire or indirect satire. The Man in Black, who frequently appears in Oliver Goldsmith's *Letters from a Citizen of the World* papers, is a Satirist who contrasts with Lien Chi Altangi, an ingénu. The King of Brobdingnag is playing the role of the Satirist when he demolishes Gulliver's panegyric on Europe in the famous invective passage ending "I cannot but conclude the Bulk of your Natives, to be the most pernicious Race of little odious Vermin that Nature ever suffered to crawl upon the Surface of the Earth."[27]

Not every Satirist exhibits all the qualities I have just described, nor is the Satirist invariably harsh and jagged. Sometimes he is gentler, professes to be moved more by pity than anger. He chides, rather than rages. This sort of Satirist we associate with the satires of Horace, as we associate his harsher brother with Juvenal. But both are recognizable as variations of the same conventional figure. Since he is a conventional figure, we should be wary about assuming that what he says can be taken literally. We should be particularly cautious about assuming that bits of what appear to be biographical or psychological information are reliable guides to the biography or psychology of the writer who has created him. Like the persona, the Satirist is essentially a character created to serve a rhetorical purpose, and his views and personality are not necessarily identical to those of his creator.

---

[26] See Ronald Paulson, "Satire in the Early Novels of Smollett", *JEGP*, LIX (1960), 381-402.
[27] *Prose Works*, XI (1959), 132.

VI

MINOR TACTICS

← Persona vs satirist. (handwritten)

The tactics discussed in Chapters III, IV, and V, although not found in every satire, seem to occur more frequently and appear to be more pervasive than those I would like to discuss in this chapter. Minor tactics, though they may be vitally important in an individual satire, are generally used for local effects.

"INDISPUTABLE" REASON

In non-satiric writing, the basis of the appeal to the reader is frequently the presentation of a logically sound argument. The reader is asked to agree, to cooperate, and to adopt a course of action because the argument is based upon sound reason. Satire frequently works in a radically different way. A course of action, an idea, or an attitude may be presented as though it were indisputably reasonable, yet instead of convincing the reader, the presentation insinuates that the ideas are unsound or, if carried to their logical extreme, pernicious. Or a set of ideas may be presented in a perfectly reasonable fashion, so reasonable that they might win our assent if we were not also made aware of the human tendencies or human values which are missing. "Reason" of this sort may thus be used not only to insinuate the blame of those who base their actions or arguments upon it, but also to attack conditions which make certain courses of action "reasonable". It may be used to insinuate the folly of currently fashionable ideas, ideals or hopes. It may also be used to emphasize the importance of the non-rational and thus to undercut man's pride in his reason.

The persona is often the vehicle of "indisputable" reason. The speaker in the elder Samuel Butler's *Satyr upon Plagaries* argues at some length that plagaries deserve a better name than they have gotten, though the reasons he gives are unlikely to convince many readers. The speaker in

The Shortest Way with the Dissenters presents the case against the Dissenters in a way which carries the demands of the High-flying Tories to a logical conclusion. The result is a *reductio ad absurdum* presentation which undermines their position. The persona in *An Argument Against Abolishing Christianity* argues in a most logical way, if one can accept his premises. Most Ingenious Critics make a great show of reaching logical conclusions upon the basis of their "evidence".

Sometimes the tactic takes the form of an argument posed more or less on the basis of formal logic, a syllogism, or a formal analogy. The persona of Swift's *Mr. Collins's Discourse of Free-Thinking* frequently argues on the basis of a patently specious analogy, and the persona of *An Argument Against Abolishing Christianity* cites with approval a long, absurd *sorites* from which a Freethinker deduces that since interpretations of Holy Writ do not agree, "I may safely whore and drink on, and defy the Parson."[1] Both the elder and younger Samuel Butler are fond of the tactic. *Hudibras* is full of chop-logic, and much of the last half of *Erewhon* consists of exhibitions of "logic" which "prove" such things as the facts that the empty pews of Erewhonian churches really indicate the piety of the Erewhonians, and vegetables have "rights" just as human beings do and therefore should not be eaten. Russell Maloney's short-story *Inflexible Logic,* to take a more modern instance, is an implicit attack upon the too literal application of the modern, logical "law of probability" outside the laboratory.

Frequently the satirist presents situations, schemes and patterns of conduct which would be reasonable under one set of circumstances, but are absurd in another. The result is to emphasize an intellectual rigidity which Bergson argued was one of the bases of comedy, as it certainly is of satire. The education of Martinus Scriblerus, for instance, is carried on according to the practice of the ancients – with ludicrous results. The March Hare's meek reply "It was the *best* butter" after greasing the works of his watch is essentially the same tactic Evelyn Waugh uses in *Black Mischief*. The Emperor Seth returns to the African kingdom of Azania fresh from a European education and proceeds to apply the latest European theories and practices to such things as the supplying of the Royal Army, control of the rapidly expanding birthrate, and reform of the monetary system. The convulsions which follow reduce the country to a barbarism worse than that before Seth's accession.

Another variation of the tactic is to have a character present a loftily

[1] *Prose Works,* II (1957), 38.

"reasonable" set of values – and then contrasts this with the way he acts when the values are put to the test. Parson Adams in *Joseph Andrews* tells Joseph that love for another human being can be carried to excess: "Now, believe me, no Christian ought so to set his heart on any person or thing in this world, but that, whenever it shall be required, or taken from him in any manner by divine Providence, he may be able, peaceably, quietly, and contentedly to resign it."[2] Immediately after, his youngest son is reported drowned and he gives way to bitter, agonized grief. Virtually the same thing happens in Chapter XVIII of *Rasselas*. The young prince has listened to a philosopher who "from the unshaken throne of rational fortitude, looks down on the scenes of life changing beneath him."[3] When he visits the philosopher later, however, he finds him in despair because his only daughter has died of a fever. O. Henry's story *A Cosmopolite in a Café* uses the same variation. A man of the world who has argued that "It'll be a better world when we quit being fools about some mildewed town or ten acres of swampland just because we happened to be born there"[4] is taken in charge by the police for defending the "honor" of his home town, Mattawamkeag, Maine.

Another variation is to carry an idea or set of conditions to a "logical", or "reasonable" conclusion. A few years ago a young mother-to-be, a Mrs. Finkbine, took thalidomide, a drug which was later discovered to have caused many children to be born deformed. She decided to have an abortion, and her decision was widely publicized. A priest wrote *Time* magazine: "As to the Finkbines' baby, if there is only a fifty-fifty chance to be normal, why not wait until he is born and kill him if he is abnormal? It would be more consequential."[5]

Thomas Love Peacock's satires are full of examples of the same device. Mr. Flosky in *Nightmare Abbey,* a character who bears a more than fortuitous resemblance to Samuel Taylor Coleridge, is characterized like this:

He had been in his youth an enthusiast for liberty, and had hailed the dawn of the French Revolution as the promise of a day that was to banish war and slavery, and every form of vice and misery, from the face of

---

[2] *The History of the Adventures of Joseph Andrews and of his Friend Mr. Abraham Adams*, Modern Library College Editions (New York, 1950), pp. 373-374.

[3] Johnson, *Rasselas, Poems, and Selected Prose*, ed. Bertrand H. Bronson (New York and Toronto, 1959), p. 546.

[4] In: *The Four Million* (New York, 1906), p. 32.

[5] *Time* (August 10, 1962), p. 3.

the earth. Because all this was not done, he deduced that nothing was done; and from this deduction, according to his system of logic, he drew a conclusion that worse than nothing was done; that the overthrow of the feudal fortresses of tyranny and superstition was the greatest calamity that had ever befallen mankind; and that their only hope now was to rake the rubbish together, and rebuild it without any of those loopholes by which the light had originally crept in.[6]

The reasoning process by which a character or group of characters reach a certain conclusion may of course be the basis of more extended episodes in satiric works. The first two chapters of *Sense and Sensibility* are a case in point. John Dashwood has inherited his father's large estate, but with the death-bed injunction that he do something hand-some for his step-mother and her three daugthers, his half-sisters. At first he is inclined to be generous and give each of the girls a thousand pounds. But as he and his wife begin to discuss the matter all sorts of objections occur. They will be robbing their young son; a thousand is too much, five hundred would be more than generous. But the girls *do* have some money already; perhaps an annuity of a hundred a year for the mother would be better. Still, their mother might live for quite a long time, and then an annuity would encourage her unduly to enlarge her standard of living. An occasional present of fifty pounds would be more than ample. More than generous, his wife agrees. Besides, she is convinced that the old man had not meant that his son should give them any money at all. An occasional present of fish and game, and such favors, was all that he really meant. Anyway, Mrs. Dashwood and her daughters had more money than they need and some most desirable furniture and plate. In any case, the old man would have left almost everything to them if he had not been prevented by the entailment. Fortified by this notion, John Dashwood comes to the conclusion that it would be "absolutely unnecessary, if not highly indecorous"[7] to do anything substantial for his relatives.

Although some reasoners are bumbling straw men whose arguments are transparent, others, like Mustapha Mond in *Brave New World* and the projector in *A Modest Proposal* argue with such force and skill that the satire seems to indict not the speaker alone, not just the party he represents, but the human tendency to separate mind and heart itself. The projector of *A Modest Proposal* argues his case for cannibalism

[6] *The Novels of Thomas Love Peacock*, edited with introductions and notes by David Garnett (London, 1948), p. 360.
[7] In: *The Complete Novels of Jane Austen*, Modern Library (New York, n.d.), p. 7.

with such mind-numbing cogency as to all but impel agreement. Mustapha Mond, a "Controller", discusses the rationale of the "Brave New
World" with John the Savage. The unpleasant things which plague the
twentieth century – want, frustration, instability – have been eliminated.
The Savage protests

"But I like the inconveniences."

"We don't," said the Controller. "We prefer to do things comfortably."

"But I don't want comfort. I want God, I want poetry, I want real
danger, I want freedom, I want goodness. I want sin."

"In fact," said Mustapha Mond, "you're claiming the right to be unhappy."

"All right then," said the Savage defiantly, "I'm claiming the right to be
unhappy."

"Not to mention the right to grow old and ugly and impotent; the right
to have syphilis and cancer; the right to have too little to eat; the right
to be lousy; the right to live in constant apprehension of what may happen
tomorrow; the right to catch typhoid; the right to be tortured by un-
speakable pains of every kind."

There was a long silence.

"I claim them all," said the Savage at last.

Mustapha Mond shrugged his shoulders. "You're welcome," he said.[8]

"Indisputable" Reason is all on the side of Mond, as it is on the side
of the projector. But it is clear that most readers are likely to prefer
something warmer and more human. They are likely to agree with
Samuel Butler's Mr. Higgs, who observes, "reason uncorrected by
instinct is as bad as instinct uncorrected by reason".[9]

Extensions of ideas, or sets of conditions may be carried much further
than they are in any of the examples just cited. They may be developed
at length and provide the basis for a long satire. *Nineteen Eighty-Four*
is based upon a logical extension of certain political conditions and
tendencies George Orwell saw in Europe in the 1930's and 1940's. The
world of 1984, the satirist seems to be saying, is the logical result of
allowing certain kinds of leaders, and certain kinds of principles, to
dominate first a party, then a nation, then the world; the world of 1984
is the result of allowing ends to ruthlessly dominate means.[10] Other
satiric novels about the "future", Evelyn Waugh's *Love Among the
Ruins,* Aldous Huxley's *Brave New World,* Sinclair Lewis' *It Can't*

---

[8]   Huxley, *Brave New World* (New York and London, 1946), p. 288.
[9]   *Erewhon and Erewhon Revisited*, p. 283.
[10]   See Emanuel Edrich, "George Orwell and the Satire in Horror", *Texas Studies
in Literature and Language*, IV (1962), 96-108.

Happen Here, are based upon similar extensions of contemporary ideas or conditions.

ASSOCIATION

A distiller who wants to create a favorable impression for his brand of whiskey shows us a well-known author taking a dram. A soft drink bottler who wants young men to drink more Coca-Cola televises a film in which Willie Mays perks himself up after a home run with a bottle of Coke. The producer of a famous line of cosmetics says simply, "She's lovely, she's engaged, she uses Pond's." In each case the manufacturer is recommending his product by using favorable associations. Products, like people, are known by the company they keep. Whiskey is associated with culture in the person of the author, Coca-Cola with the virility and athletic glamor of a baseball star. These associations are implicit, whether or not they have been underlined by a verbal comment. The Pond's slogan carries the process a step further. The lady who uses Pond's is associated with physical beauty and with the pleasant and desirable state of being engaged, and the association is pointed up by the syntactical equivalence of "lovely", "engaged", and "uses Pond's".

Association is a basic satiric tactic and sometimes works in a way directly contrary to the one our advertisers are using. That is, the writer of the satire works upon the assumption that the members of his audience will feel that some things are blameworthy. (The feelings of course are part of the Context in which the satire operates.) These things may be ideas, people, certain kinds of objects – in fact any things which can evoke an unfavorable response. The satirist thus may insinuate blame simply by associating or identifying the object of the satire with things which his audience will dislike, fear, or think morally repugnant. The effect is to include the object of the satire in the opprobrium – to blame by association.[11] In perhaps its most basic – though not necessarily least complex – form, the association is made by listing and juxtaposing a number of items. The following are typical:

Nouns of number, or multitude, such as *Mob*, Parliament, Rabble, House of Commons, Regiment, Court of King's Bench, Den of Thieves, and the like. William Cobbett[12]

---

[11] Though for simplicity's sake I have called the tactic "association", some associations are in effect implied or expressed analogies, others similes or metaphors.
[12] *English Grammar, Letter xvii, Syntax as Relating to Pronouns,* quoted in *The Oxford Dictionary of Quotations* (Oxford, 1941), p. 97.

My Reconcilement to the *Yahoo*-kind in general might not be so difficult, if they would be content with those Vices and Follies only which Nature hath Intitled them to. I am not in the least provoked at the Sight of a Lawyer, a Pick-pocket, a Colonel, a Fool, a Lord, a Gamester, a Politician, a Whoremunger, a Physician, an Evidence, a Suborner, an Attorney, a Traitor, or the like: This is all according to the due Course of Things . . .[13].

Gulliver, in *Gulliver's Travels*, Part IV

To say 'I accept' in an age like our own is to say that you accept concentration camps, rubber truncheons, Hitler, Stalin, bombs, aeroplanes, tinned food, machine guns, putsches, purges, slogans, Bedaux belts, gas masks, submarines, spies, provocateurs, press censorship, secret prisons, aspirins, Hollywood films, and political murders.[14]

George Orwell, in *"Inside the Whale"*

> There mark what ills the scholar's life assail,
> Toil, envy, want, the patron, and the jail.[15]

Samuel Johnson, *The Vanity of Human Wishes*

The insinuation inherent in lists like these appears to be the result not only of association, but of several factors operating together. At first glance the separate items appear incongruous; they apparently belong to different moral orders. But their association insinuates that despite the apparent dissimilarity we should see underlying similarity or unity. We would not be so likely to think that there was something soul-destroying and vicious about "aspirin" and "Hollywood films" if Orwell had not placed them in such bad company, nor would we have such an unfavorable opinion of lawyers and colonels if they were mentioned in other contexts. The suggestion of unity is strengthened by the syntax. A syntactical equivalence implies other sorts of equivalences. Finally, the juxtaposition of at least some of the items is insinuating. Gulliver pairs each profession with a vice or folly which suggests a connection with the profession. Moreover, "Colonel" is preceded by "Pick-pocket" and followed by "Fool", a suggestion that a Colonel may be something of both. Johnson not only lists "patron" with the more obvious "ills" which afflict the scholar's life, he juxtaposes "patron" between "want" and "jail", a juxtaposition which may suggest more narrowly that a patron insures neither comfort nor freedom for the scholar.

In the examples I have just cited, the associations were made by a speaker to reflect upon something else. The speaker may be a persona, like Gulliver in the second example, and, if so, he is for the moment at

---

[13] *Prose Works*, XI (1959), 296.
[14] *Inside the Whale and Other Essays* (Harmondsworth, Middlesex, 1962), p. 17.
[15] *Rasselas, Poems, and Selected Prose*, p. 51, ll. 159-160.

least the vehicle for, rather than the object of, the insinuation. Swift is fond of having his personas use the tactic. Gulliver uses it to attack free-thinkers in Part IV of *Gulliver's Travels* where they are associated with "Begging, Robbing ... Pimping ... Whoring ...."[16] and in *An Argument Against Abolishing Christianity* the persona associates two free-thinkers, Toland and Tindal, with the Roman Catholic Church. Thus Toland is "an *Irish* priest, the son of an *Irish* priest", and Tindal "was, in a proper Juncture, reconciled to the *Romish Faith*; whose true Son, as appears by an Hundred Passages in his Treatise, he still continues".[17]

Association may be used somewhat differently, as the following brief examples will suggest:

[Mrs. Kernan] believed steadily in the Sacred Heart as the most generally useful of all Catholic devotions and approved of the sacraments. Her faith was bounded by her kitchen, but, if she was put to it, she could believe also in the banshee and in the Holy Ghost.[18]

James Joyce, "Grace", *Dubliners*

Here Files of Pins extend their shining Rows,
Puffs, Powders, Patches, Bibles, Billet-doux.[19]

The Rape of the Lock

In the first group of examples the insinuation was directed at certain items on the lists themselves. Outside the satire some would have been blameworthy, some not; the association itself suggested an equivalence. In the quotations from Joyce and Pope a second kind of insinuation by association is operating. In these the insinuation seems to inhere in the fact, not that some items are more blameworthy than others, but that things from different levels of seriousness, or different moral orders, are associated on a more or less equal basis (this is made clear by the syntactical equivalence of the items). This kind of association insinuates a moral failing, not in the things themselves but in those who, we are told or led to believe, make the association.

Joyce insinuates that Mrs. Kernan associates and makes equivalents of the banshee and the Holy Ghost, implying that her religious faith is naive, undiscriminating, and suffused with folk superstition. Mentioning the Holy Ghost and the banshee is simply one way of doing this, and almost any similar pair would have served as well. In Pope's line "Bibles" is associated and made the equivalent of "Puffs", "Powders",

---

[16] *Prose Works*, XI (1959), 252.
[17] *Prose Works*, II (1957), 37.
[18] *Modern Library* (New York, n.d.), p. 200.
[19] *Poems*, 3rd ed., II, 156. (Canto I, ll. 137-138.)

"Patches", and "Billet-doux". This suggests a number of insinuations. "Bibles" may be, like "Powders" and "Patches", items of adornment for a young lady of fashion. They may have been, like "Billet-doux", sent by admirers, or used as concealments for the admirers' letters. The juxtaposition between two different classes of things suggests that either or both of these interpretations is possible. Or the equivalence may more simply insinuate a similar, blameworthy equivalence in the mind of their admirer. Whatever the case, the target is Belinda, and young ladies like her.[20]

In both of these examples, the insinuating association is made by the narrator of the satire. A persona may of course associate himself with things which are absurdly vain, morally dispicable, or otherwise discreditable, thus blackening his own character, or the characters of those he represents. The elder Samuel Butler does this in his "Character" *A Modern Politician* which I quoted earlier. The politician associates himself with the angels. "Henry Garnet", a persona in John Oldham's vigorous *Satires upon the Jesuits* undercuts his character and that of his order with a radically different set of associations. The poem was written in 1679 when public feeling ran high against Catholics in general and the Jesuits in particular as a result of the so-called Popish Plot. The "Ghost" of Henry Garnet, an English Jesuit who had been executed in 1606 for complicity in the Gunpowder Plot, is represented addressing the Jesuits just after the murder of Sir Edmund Berry Godfrey, the magistrate who had taken Titus Oates' deposition.

"By hell", Garnet begins, " 'twas bravely done! what less than this,/ What sacrifice of meaner worth, and price/ Could we have offered up for our success?"[21] "By hell" is an appropriate beginning, for in the address which follows Garnet proudly associates the Jesuits with blood sacrifice, with Cataline, the Roman conspiritor against the state, with the regicides who had killed Charles I, with Clement and Ravaillac, the murderers of the French kings Henry III and Henry IV, with Nero, and with Lucifer himself. The latter association is particularly significant, for Garnet regards his Jesuits and the Church they serve as an earthly branch of Hell. This is clear in the association with which the following lines end:

[20] In verse satire associations are of course frequently suggested, or pointed up, by internal rime ("land of Abraham Lincoln and Lydia E. Pinkham" – E. E. Cummings, *Poem, or Beauty Hurts Mr. Vinal*) or end rime ("And shewn your *Presbyterian* wits/ Jump punctual with the Jesuits." – *Hudibras*, III, i, 499-500).
[21] *Poems of John Oldham*, with an introduction by Bonamy Dobrée (London, 1960), p. 85.

Think on that matchless assassin, whose name
We with just pride can make our happy claim;
He, who at the killing of an emperor,
To give his poison greater force and power
Mixed a god with 't, and made it work more sure:
Blessed memory! which shall through age to come
Stand sacred in the lists of hell and Rome.[22]

In *Mr. Collins's Discourse of Free-Thinking* Swift uses association in a more complicated way. The tract, published in 1713 and intended to ridicule the famous free-thinker Anthony Collins, was ostensibly prepared by a *"Friend of the* Author" who in his introduction associates himself and Collins with the Whig party, with anarchy, and what he calls "Atheology". In the *Discourse of Free-Thinking* itself, which the "friend" has prepared as an abstract of Collins's ideas, Collins is made to cite an eminent list of "Free Thinkers" including not only the great pagan philosophers, but Solomon, Origen, the "Prophets of the *Old Testament"*, who, the reader is assured, "were generally *Free Thinkers",* and the late Archbishop of Canterbury.[23] The associations are so far-fetched, of course, that they reflect adversely upon Collins.

In the examples cited above, most of the contemporary audience to which these satires were addressed would have brought unfavorable ideas or feelings about such things as "Whoring", "Roman Catholics", "Whigs", "Atheology", and so on TO the satire. The satirist had only to exploit the unfavorable connotations already established. However, he may also establish unfavorable connotations WITHIN a satire and then associate the object of the attack with them. Pope uses this tactic skillfully in his *Guardian* essay Number 40 to ridicule Ambrose Philips' pastorals. Philips is associated with Spenser – not with Spenser generally, or with Spenser's pastorals as a whole, for Pope could scarcely do this without implying a favorable judgment, but with what are made to seem the worst features of Spenser's pastorals, their inconsistency and inelegant diction. Having established this association, Pope goes a step further. He invents a writer of bad pastorals, and says Philips has "hit into the same Road" as this "old *West Country* Bard"[24] whose poem, the author solemnly assures the reader, he has found in some old manuscripts. The old Bard's pastoral, a sample of which is quoted,

[22] *Poems*, p. 86. See Cooper R. Mackin's useful "The Satiric Technique of John Oldham's *Satyrs Upon the Jesuits*", *SP*, LXII (1965), 78-90.
[23] *Prose Works*, IV (1957), 45.
[24] *Prose Works*, p. 106.

is a parody of the worst features of Philips' own pastoral poems.

When the reader comes to the satire with ideas, attitudes, feelings which may work against a satiric association or identification, the satirist must block off, or keep in the background, ideas which will confuse him, or blunt the point of the attack. He may do this as Pope has done by simply not mentioning good features. Pope is careful to let the reader know that he is associating Philips with only one aspect of Spenser's pastorals. Associating Philips with Spenser generally would have spoiled, or at least considerably confused, the point he is making.

Robert Burns, in his *Address to the Deil,* boldly chooses the opposite course. He begins by quoting *Paradise Lost* to conjure up the awesome "Deil" most of his readers will imagine:

> O Prince! O Chief of many thronèd pow'rs!
> That led th' embattl'd seraphim to war –

Then immediately undercuts the somber and mighty figure of Satan by parodying Milton, and addressing the Deil with an easy-going, patronizing familiarity:

> O Thou! whatever title suit thee –
> Auld Hornie, Satan, Nick, or Clootie –
> Wha in yon cavern grim an' sootie,
>   Clos'd under hatches,
> Spairges about the brunstane cootie,
>   To scaud poor wretches![25]

The fearsome figure of Satan effectively toppled from his pedestal, Burns can proceed with the business of the poem – satirizing the Calvinist hell-fire preachers' Devil by identifying him with the familiar witches, hob-goblins, and water-sprites of the Scottish countryside.

Not only may a satirist stigmatize by association, he may also do the reverse – that is, insinuate blame by pointedly REFUSING to associate praiseworthy persons or things with what he wants to attack. In *Headlong Hall,* Peacock tells us Squire Harry Headlong "became seized with a violent passion to be thought a philosopher and a man of taste; and accordingly set off on an expedition to Oxford, to inquire for other varieties of the same genera, namely, men of taste and philosophers; but, being assured by a learned professor that there were no such things in the University, he proceeded to London . . .".[26] In the 1720's a proposal was made to establish a Bank of Ireland. Swift was one of its

---

[25]   *Poems,* p. 108.
[26]   *The Novels of Thomas Love Peacock,* p. 10.

opponents. In a paper Herbert Davis attributes to him, the following list of supporters of the proposal is given:

NOBILITY

Arch Bishops	0
Marquisses	0
Earls	0
Viscounts	3
Barons	1
Bishops	2
French Baron	*1*

A note following says "N. B. The Temporal Lords of *Ireland* are 125, the Bishops 22. In all 147, Exclusive of the aforesaid *French* Count."[27] Since none of the highest temporal or spiritual lords and few of the lower were willing to support the proposal, the satirist's point is clear.

The satirist may also emphasize two contrasting scales of values, pointedly associating the object of the satire with the inferior one and disassociating it from the superior. In *Mac Flecknoe*, for instance, Dryden associates Shadwell not only with Flecknoe himself, but with Heywood, Shirley and Dekker, whose reputations were low during the Restoration, and dissociates him from the much-admired Fletcher and Jonson. Evelyn Waugh in *The Loved One* uses a variation of the same tactic. Dennis Barlow, the "hero" of the novel, has been courting a young California lady, Aimée Thanatogenos, with poems culled from *The Oxford Book of English Verse*. Dennis finds that they have not had the effect he hoped for:

The English poets were proving uncertain guides in the labyrinth of Californian courtship – nearly all were too casual, too despondent, too ceremonious, or too exacting; they scolded, they pleaded, they extolled. Dennis required salesmanship; he sought to present Aimée with an irresistible picture not so much of her own merits or even of his, as of the enormous gratification he was offering. The films did it; the crooners did it; but not, it seemed, the English poets.[28]

Another variant is to combine praise and blame. Something with a favorable connotation is dissociated from the object of the satire and associated with its contrary. In a passage from *Satires upon the Jesuits,* an example in point, Oldham has "Garnet's Ghost" disassociate the

---

27 *Prose Works*, IX (1948), 288.
28 (Harmondsworth, Middlesex), p. 84.

Jesuits from religion and the Bible and associate both with their enemies. Garnet begins this passage by asking the Jesuits what deters them
from killing the king:

> what is't that binds your hands? does fear
> From such a glorious action you deter?
> Or is't religion? but you sure disclaim
> That frivolous pretence, that empty name –
> Mere bugbear word, devised by us to scare
> The senseless rout to slavishness and fear,
> Ne'er known to awe the brave, and those that dare.
> Such weak and feeble things may serve for checks
> To rein and curb base mettled heretics;
> Dull creatures, whose nice boggling consciences
> Startle, or strain at such slight crimes as these;
> Such, whom fond inbred honesty befools,
> Or that old musty piece the Bible gulls:
> That hated book, the bulwark of our foes,
> Whereby they still uphold their tottering cause.[29]

The tactic may be used in still more complex ways, as Pope does
in the following passage of the *Epistle to Dr. Arbuthnot*. He begins by
arguing that there are worse things than having powerful enemies:

> – One Flatt'rer's worse than all;
> Of all mad Creatures, if the Learn'd are right,
> It is the Slaver kills, and not the Bite.
> A Fool quite angry is quite innocent;
> Alas! 'tis ten times worse when they *repent*.
>
> One dedicates, in high Heroic prose,
> And ridicules beyond a hundred foes;
> One from all *Grubstreet* will my fame defend,
> And, more abusive, calls himself my friend.
> This prints my Letters, that expects a Bribe,
> And others roar aloud, "Subscribe, subscribe."
> There are, who to my Person pay their court,
> I cough like *Horace,* and tho' lean, am short,
> *Ammon's* great Son one shoulder had too high,
> Such Ovid's nose, and "Sir! you have an *Eye*–"
> Go on, obliging Creatures, make me see
> All that disgrac'd my Betters, met in me:
> Say for my comfort, languishing in bed,
> "Just so immortal *Maro* held his head:"
> And when I die, be sure you let me know
> Great *Homer* dy'd three thousand years ago.[30]

29 *Poems of John Oldham,* p. 88.
30 *Poems,* 2nd ed., IV, 103-104, ll. 104-124.

We might paraphrase as follows: Pope pictures himself afflicted by flattering fools. They attempt to associate themselves with him by calling him friend, by praising him, by performing various unsolicited literary services. They associate him with the honored ancients by calling attention to trivial and demeaning physical similarities. Pope identifies the fools with mad dogs, whose slobbering friendly advances are more deadly than attacks with their teeth. He contempuously dissociates himself from them.

SELECTION, CONCENTRATION, ACCENTUATION

The editors of a newspaper can produce a "crime wave" overnight simply by selecting all the stories of murders, muggings, knifings, and concentrating them in one page, or one section of the newspaper. The editors need make no explicit comment – concentration in itself will suggest that crime is on the increase whether or not this is the case. Similarly, a satirist may produce a satiric effect by isolating and bringing together certain kinds of material. The individual items may be relatively innocuous; concentrated, however, they will carry a weight and produce an impression that the items individually do not.

Swift, in *A Compleat Collection of Genteel and Ingenious Conversation,* uses the tactics in their purest form. The work is a long dialogue among various members of the *beau monde*, caught in their daily round of fashionable activities. Mr. Neverout, a gentleman of fashion, and Colonel Atwit meet and rally Miss Notable in Lady Smart's antechamber in an early passage:

[*Miss* Notable *comes in.*]
Nev. Miss, your Slave; I hope your early Rising will do you no Harm: I find you are but just come out of the *Cloth-Market.*
Miss. I always rise at Eleven, whether it be Day or no.
Col. Miss, I hope you're up for all Day.
Miss. Yes, if I don't get a Fall before Night.
Col. Miss, I heard you were out of Order. Pray how are you now?
Miss. Pretty well Colonel, I thank you.
Col. Pretty, and Well, Miss, that's two very good Things.
Miss. I mean, I am better than I was.
Nev. Why, then 'tis well you were sick.
Miss. What, Mr. *Neverout,* you take me up, before I'm down.[31]

The separate elements of the dialogue apparently needed only to be

---

[31]   *Prose Works*, IV (1957), 132-133.

transcribed from life; indeed, many of the clichés are still current in much the same form that Swift took them down. Reported separately, the effect would be negligible – concentrated and put into the form of a dialogue, they are an effective satiric thrust at a "polite society" in which clichés were used to "conceal ignorance or stupidity, or to prevent the labour of thoughts to produce native sentiment, and combine such words as will precisely express it".[32] Samuel Johnson used the same tactics in *The Idler* papers on Dick Minim, the critic whose critical precepts are a collection of truisms current at the time, as does the contemporary writer Frank Sullivan in his "cliché expert" series.

E. B. White uses a somewhat different variation in "About Myself", an essay which appeared in *The New Yorker* during the Second World War. He begins:

I am a man of medium height. I keep my records in a Weis Folder Re-order Number 8003. The unpaid balance of my estimated tax for the year 1945 is item 3 less the sum of items 4 and 5. My eyes are gray. My Selective Service order number is 10789. The serial number is T1654. I am in Class IV-A, and have been variously in Class 3-A, Class 1-A(H), and Class 4-H. My social security number is 067-01-9841. I am married to U. S. Woman Number 067-01-9807. Her eyes are gray. This is not a joint declaration, nor is it made by an agent; therefore it need be signed only by me – and, as I said, I am a man of medium height.

The remainder of the essay is like this. It is a concentrated accounting of the forms, the numbers, the interminable, life-stifling paperwork which was inescapable during the war. The concentration is sufficient to make the point The human being has become a statistical abstraction identified by figures, controlled by forms. It ends:

I owe a letter to Corporal 32413654, Hq, and Hq Sq., VII AAF S. C., APO 953, c/o PM San Francisco, Calif., thanking him for the necktie he sent me at Christmas. In 1918 I was a private in the Army. My number was 4,345,016. I was a boy of medium height. I had light hair. I had no absences from duty under G. O. 31, 1912, or G. O. 45, 1914. The number of that war was Number One.[33]

W. H. Auden's poem "The Unknown Citizen" has some strong similarities. The poem is a eulogy to "JS/07/M/378" whose "Marble Monument" is being erected by the State. The speaker, presumably a spokesman for the State, lists the qualities which have endeared this perfectly normal "unknown citizen" to his leaders. We see that he was

---

[32] Note to the Dublin edition of 1738, in *Satires and Personal Writings by Jonathan Swift*, ed. William Alfred Eddy (London and New York, 1933), p. 195.
[33] In: *The Second Tree from the Corner*, pp. 73, 76.

a statistically predictable employee, consumer, and familyman. Detail after detail adds to the evidence. What the State values least, and what has been left out of the accounting is implied by the questions with which the poem ends: "Was he free? Was he happy? The question is absurd:/ Had anything been wrong, we should certainly have heard."[34]

In the examples I have cited thus far, the effect seems to be produced largely by selection and concentration; frequently, however, the items are not only selected and concentrated, but exaggerated as well. Pope's *Spectator* essay Number 452 is a satire on the trivia appearing in current newspapers, and the public's uncritical appetite for it. He proposes a new newspaper to be devoted exclusively to tit-bits of trivial information, and quotes half-a-dozen examples of the sort of news the paper will contain — news from Paddington that a sow-gelder has recently passed through, from Fulham that "a Tub of excellent Ale"[35] has just been broached at Parsons Green, and so on.

Pope shapes the individual items; Swift, more subtly, shapes the entire treatise in *A Tritical Essay upon the Faculties of the Mind*. This is a collection of "tritical" (*i.e.,* trite) philosophical saws presented as a model for the imitation of young writers. The clichés themselves are presented much as Swift might have noted them in conversation or reading, and he has made the treatise as a whole meandering, shapeless, digressive, and his persona hardly touches upon the subject he has set for himself. The effect is not only to imply that "philosophical" writers do not think for themselves, but that they are incapable even of elementary ordering and coherence.

Sometimes the satirist collects and concentrates all the ridiculous or bad features of a literary genre and presents them as the "right" way to create a great, or successful, work of art. This is Pope's tactic in his *Guardian* essay Number 78 (later called *A Receipt To Make an Epic Poem* when it was adapted as Chapter Fifteen of *Peri Bathous*). The persona advocates indiscriminate pillaging of "any old Poem, History-book, Romance, or Legend"[36] for the fable, episodes, manners, machines, and descriptions of the new epic and mixing them in a recipe which will insure a "grand Performance". The *Letter of Advice to a Young Poet,* often attributed to Swift, employs the same tactics — the objectionable features of Grub Street poetry are collected and praised,

[34] *Modern American and Modern British Poetry*, ed. Louis Untermeyer (revised, shorter edition; New York and Burlingame, 1955), p. 637.
[35] *Prose Works*, p. 58.
[36] *The Art of Sinking in Poetry: Martinus Scriblerus' Peri Bathous*, ed. Edna Leake Steeves (New York, 1952), p. 81.

and the persona advocates that his young correspondent adopt them if he would achieve success in letters. The same variation may be used for other purposes as well. Benjamin Franklin, in his essay *Rules by Which a Great Empire May be Reduced to a Small One* poses as a "modern simpleton" who has gathered together all the ways by which colonies and dependencies may be brought to hate and fear the mother country. He presents them to "all ministers who have the management of extensive dominions, which from their very greatness are become troublesome to govern, because the multiplicity of their affairs leaves no time for *fiddling*".[37]

Listing and repetition of various kinds are allied to concentration, for the effect of these tactics depends not only upon the individual items, but upon an accumulation of detail: the satiric effect of the whole is greater than the sum of the individual parts. Lists of projects, like those in Part III of *Gulliver's Travels*, or in the elder Samuel Butler's *Satyr upon the Royal Society*, the list of devices for achieving the bathetic in *Peri Bathous*, the list of absurd "works" at the beginning of *A Tale of a Tub*, the "*Discoveries and Works of the Great Scriblerus*" at the end of the *Memoirs of Martinus Scriblerus* – all are absurd not only because the individual items are absurd, but because the very length of the list intensifies the effect.

Repetition may have much the same effect. Repeated use of footnotes, for example, may point an attack upon pedantry. Frequently the contents of the notes are insinuating as well, but the repetition itself is suggestive. Repeated use of certain kinds of words may have an insinuating effect. Many satires contain relatively high proportions of words drawn from a single area of activity. *The Beggar's Opera* is full of underworld cant, *The Canon's Yeoman's Tale*, alchemical terms, and *Brave New World*, scientific terminology. Repetition and concentration of terms like these gives them a slight satiric charge since they are a constant reminder of the direction of the satiric attack. The satirist may give repeated examples of absurdities – often absurdities based upon a single irrationality which appears in various guises. The absurd projects in Book III of *Gulliver's Travels* and the elder Butler's *Satyr upon the Royal Society* as well as the remarkable educational schemes in *Martinus Scriblerus* derive a good deal of their force from repetition. In longer satires an idea or theme may recur time and again in various guises, each repetition adding to the cumulative force of the

---

[37] In *Classic Essays in English*, ed. Josephine Miles (Boston and Toronto, 1961), p. 105.

satire. In *Gulliver's Travels* the evils of conquest, and of war in general, the ruthlessness of absolute power, the invincibility and complacency of ignorance, man's present debasement in comparison with an earlier and better state – these ideas appear time after time, though always in a slightly different guise.[38] In *A Tale of a Tub,* abundant varieties of irrationality occur, and in Melville's *The Confidence-Man,* repeated examples of the folly of mindless optimism. Terry Southern's *The Magic Christian* consists of one anecdote after another demonstrating the brutalizing effect of money; Nigel Dennis' *Cards of Identity* presents one wry example after another of the difficulty of establishing and maintaining an identity. Satiric themes like these recur like leitmotifs, help to unify rather episodic works, and are at least a partial explanation of their satiric power.

A satiric point may be scored not only by listing or repeating, but by stretching something to an inordinate length – thus forcing the audience to dwell upon it – and the very fact that something is dwelt upon in a satiric context is often enough to insinuate blame. Chaucer's *Tale of Melibee* seems unduly long – this, and the fact that it follows *Sir Thopas* suggests at least that Chaucer may be making a satiric point.

Accentuation, or exaggeration, which I mentioned above, is usually employed in conjunction with selection and concentration. It can occur in relative isolation, however. Sandy Wilson's post-war musical play *The Boy Friend,* which re-created plot situations, characters, and types of music which had been popular in the 1920's, was received by London audiences as a slightly sentimental piece, by New York audiences as a somewhat satirical one. Part of the difference was due to the different context the audience brought to the play, part to relatively slight accentuation of the absurdities of the situations by the actors.

The subtlest forms of accentuation are mostly oral, for the human voice may suggest by the slightest change of inflection, the slightest dwelling upon a word, a satiric meaning which would be lost in print. One of the reasons why Chaucer is among the subtlest satirists in English may be that many of his works were designed to be delivered orally. Satirists who work largely by accentuation are usually oral satirists, and their satire may lose much if it is transferred to print. Mike Nichols and Elaine May, for instance, are brilliantly satiric when they can be heard, but their satire loses much of its point on the printed page.

---

[38] Discussed in Ellen Douglass Leyburn, *Satiric Allegory: Mirror of Man,* Yale Studies in English, CXXX (New Haven, 1956), pp. 88-91.

One way of course of attempting to transfer verbal inflections to the printed page is by punctuation. The fact that a word is followed by an exclamation point where none seems called for, that it is set in italic, or other unusual type, or capitalized when it would not normally be, may serve to suggest an insinuation. Quotation marks, too, may be used to insinuate. A psychiatrist writing to the *Los Angeles Times* complained that Harold Gray, the creator of Orphan Annie, used quotation marks around words like "treatment", "examination", and "mentally ill" and inferred, probably quite rightly, that Gray was insinuating "a rather hostile attitude toward the psychiatric profession".[39] *Sic* may be used to imply a fault which would not be obvious otherwise. It is sometimes used in place of an insinuating exclamation point, or as the printed equivalent of a sardonic cocking of an eyebrow, or a sly inflection of the satirist's voice implying "*This* is what the dolt says. You and I, reader, know better."

Selection, concentration, and accentuation are tactics central to parody, and it is not surprising that some of the works I have cited above suggest parody even when no original of the parody is known. The tactics often involve quoting or citing incidents out of context. In cases like these, they are used in conjunction with a direct or insinuating commentary which points up or puts the concentrated material in perspective. Swift's attack upon the deist Anthony Collins, *Mr. Collins's Discourse of Free-Thinking,* which I mentioned earlier, belongs to this category. Swift adopts the persona of a friend of Collins who enthusiastically adopts his views and quotes from Collins' *Discourse of Free-Thinking.* The quotations out of context, and the friend's enthusiastic development of Collin's arguments, reduce both the original work, and Collins himself, to absurdity. One of Thomas Love Peacock's favorite devices is similar – in novels like *Nightmare Abbey* and *Headlong Hall* he selects, concentrates and accentuates the absurdities of contemporaries whom he clothes in the thinnest of disguises and, in effect, makes them parody themselves.

Parodies of literary works of course are based upon the same tactics. In close parodies of a single work, selection and concentration are scarcely necessary; accentuation alone is sufficient. If the parody is based upon, not a single work, but upon a group of them, or a style in general, selection and concentration are likely to be employed as well. The existence of a collection of parodies like Dwight Macdonald's

[39] *Los Angeles Times* (February 9, 1965), Part II, p. 4.

Parodies: An Anthology from Chaucer to Beerbohm – and After makes exemplification unnecessary. Almost any page of Mr. Macdonald's fine anthology will provide good examples.

CONTRASTS

Since satiric tactics are essentially ways of making deviations from a norm seem blameworthy, contrast between a norm and the object of the satire, or contrast which in some other way insinuates a blameworthy deviation from a norm, plays a part in nearly all the tactics which I have discussed above. However, contrast is such a basic device that I should like to discuss it a little further, even at the expense of occasionally repeating, focussing this time on the ways in which contrast is used within a satire to establish, or to enforce, a satiric point.

1. *Diction*

One kind of contrast is established and enforced by the diction of the satire. The satirist insinuates his meaning by applying a kind of language to a subject which is not normally used to describe it. A village girl may be described as courtly poets describe a great lady, or a lady at her dressing table as though she were a priestess at an altar. A Puritan knight might be described in low colloquial terms. It is customary to divide these contrasts between diction and subject into "high" and "low" burlesque. (The terms cover other kinds of tactics as well, but diction is a constant, important element in both.) We say that a satirist is writing high burlesque when he uses elevated diction to describe something which is patently less dignified and low burlesque when he describes a fairly serious subject in low, mean terms. Perhaps the most obvious, and common effect of many of these passages is the ridicule of the object of the satire by denying it dignity, as in a low burlesque like *Hudibras*, or insinuation by using elevated diction and standards of value by comparison with which the object of the satire seems petty or contemptible, as in a high burlesque like *Mac Flecknoe*.[40]

---

[40]   Analogous effects may of course be gained by certain kinds of meter and rime. The jigging meter of *Sir Thopas*, of much of *Hudibras*, of many of Swift's satiric poems – to mention only a few familiar examples – help diminish the objects of the satires by denying them dignity, and the doubled or trebled fantastic rimes which are so noticeable in Butler and Byron, and in Swift, whom Byron acknowledged as one of his masters, ridicule the matter conveyed in them by serving the

However, not all contrasts between language and subject work so simply. An apparent incongruity may have the paradoxical effect of suggesting a partial, but nonetheless genuine *congruity*. Cleanth Brooks points out that Belinda is celebrated as well as satirized in *The Rape of the Lock,* and a successful reading of the poem must take both insinuations into account.[41] In some satires, moreover, what appears to be an incongruity may be a means of suggesting a similarity which might be the real point of the satire. To take a contemporary instance, in Peter de Vries' *The Mackerel Plaza* the clergyman-narrator describes his church like this:

Our church is, I believe, the first split-level church in America. It has five rooms and two baths downstairs – dining area, kitchen and three parlors for committee and group meetings – with a crawl space behind the furnace ending in the hillside into which the structure is built. Upstairs is one huge all-purpose interior, divisible into different-sized components by means of sliding walls and convertible into an auditorium for putting on plays, a gymnasium for athletics, and a ballroom for dances. There is a small worship area at one end.[42]

Terms which are normally used to describe a suburban home are used to describe a church, and there is of course an incongruity implicit. Yet the impression of incongruity is only momentary, for while the terms are startling and amusing, they point to a basic, blameworthy similarity. The Reverend Mackerel's church is really quite well-adapted to being used for modern living and recreation. It is only indifferently suited to the traditional purposes of worship.

One of the sequences in William Faulkner's *The Hamlet* is another instance of the difficulty of making neat distinctions. In Book Three the narrator describes a love-affair between the idiot, Ike Snopes, and a cow. Ike falls passionately in love with the animal, rescues it from a fire which threatens its life and instinctively rejects the money with which the cow's owner has tried to reward him. A little later he steals the cow and runs away with it. Grotesque as the whole series of events is, it is patterned upon a typical sequence familiar in romance. Ike is an adoring lover who proves the worth of his love with a valiant deed. He

same negative purpose that undignified meters do. The measured, frequently stately meters of some of Dryden's and Pope's satires are familiar examples of a contrary effect: their very elevation and dignity insinuate a comment about the matter contained in them.

[41] In: "The Case of Miss Arabella Fermor", *The Well Wrought Urn* (New York, 1947), pp. 80-104.

[42] (New York, 1959), p. 10.

rejects a material reward for the deed and finally, like young Lochinvar and the heroes of a hundred romances, steals his lady and flees with her. Faulkner never lets us forget the sheer grotesqueness of the passage, but constantly suggests a heroic and romantic frame of reference as well. A good part of this romantic frame of reference is carried by a consciously heightened style, but there are frequently also more specific suggestions. When Ike saves the cow from the fire he must first face a fear-maddened horse "stooping at him", the "fierce dragon-reek of its passage, blasting at his hair and garments . . .".[43] When Ike watches the sunrise the morning after their flight the narrator says:

> Now he watches the recurrence of that which he discovered for the first time three days ago: that dawn, light, is not decanted onto earth from the sky, but instead is from the earth itself suspired. Roofed by the woven canopy of blind annealing grass-roots and the roots of trees, dark in the blind dark of time's silt and rich refuse – the constant and unslumbering anonymous worm-glut and the inextricable known bones – Troy's Helen and the nymphs and the snoring mitred bishops, the saviors and the victims and the kings – it wakes, up-seeping, attritive in uncountable creeping channels . . . .
>
> (p. 184)

When Ike returns to the cow in the evening the narrator returns to the same theme:

> He walks lightly upon it [the earth], returning, treading lightly that frail inextricable canopy of the subterrene slumber – Helen and the bishops, the kings and the graceless seraphim.
>
> (p. 189)

There is of course a comic incongruity in this, as there is in virtually all such contrasts. Yet there is an underlying congruity too and upon it the satiric effect of the passage depends. Grotesque, even repulsive as it is, Ike's love is genuinely selfless and true. Thus there is a certain appropriateness in conjuring up a frame of reference in which Ike's passion is associated with high romance. But this, I presume, is not the main point. Ike's unfortunate passion for the cow is the only example of perfectly selfless love in the novel; it therefore seems intended to suggest, outlandish as it is, a norm which none of the others reach.

2. *Puns and Re-Definitions*

Some contrasts are developed at some length, as are many of those I have cited above. However, a single word may be enough to make a

[43]   (New York, 1940), p. 175.

satiric point. The satirist may pun-with-a purpose – that is, use a word with two or more meanings, one meaning conveying something innocuous or even praiseworthy about the object of the satire, the other insinuating blame. The speaker in "The General Prologue" to *The Canterbury Tales* remarks that the Pardoner "was in chirche a noble ecclesiaste" (76). One meaning of "noble" suggests the Pardoner's outward appearance and deportment. He appears to be a praiseworthy ecclesiastic. But "noble" is also the name of a gold coin and this second meaning implies something about the Pardoner's reasons for preaching. Pope's famous lines on Bentley contain the same tactic: "Where Bentley late tempestuous wont to sport/ In troubled waters, but now sleeps in Port." [44] As F. R. Leavis says, "Bentley is both the Leviathan resting in sheltered waters after majestic play and the befuddled don dozing." [45] The contrasting dual meanings of "noble" and "port" lay ready to the satirist's hand as it were; the art lies in seeing their possibilities and fitting them into a context in which both meanings contribute to the satiric effect.

A related, and considerably more common verbal tactic, is to "redefine", or "refine" the meaning of a word or phrase in such a way that one meaning, the one that is essential to the satiric effect, is paramount. In effect, the satiric meaning blots out the other meanings and carries a satiric charge within the satire which contrasts with its "normal" meaning. Words of this sort can be roughly classified by noting the amount of manipulation necessary to re-define them.

The first group consists of words which have emotionally neutral denotations, but equivocal connotations. One set of connotations is innocuous or favorable, the other discreditable. Hence in a non-satiric context words like these can be used without insinuating blame, but in a satiric context they need little manipulation to insinuate something blameworthy about the object of the satire. During the eighteenth century words like "projector", "candour",[46] and "enthusiast", and phrases like "great man" belonged to the group. Similar modern terms are "appease", "liquidate", and "politician", if the latter has not already passed beyond the pale and become a term of frank abuse. The meanings of words like this shift, even within a fairly short period of time.

---

[44] *Poems*, 3rd ed., V, 362, ll. 201-202.
[45] *Revaluation: Tradition and Development in English Poetry* (London, 1959), p. 97.
[46] See Mary Claire Randolph, " 'Candour' in XVIIIth-century Satire", *Review of English Studies*, XX (1944), 45-62.

They are natural elements of a satirist's vocabulary simply because they are so easily charged with insinuation.

A second group consists of words whose denotations and connotations both are relatively neutral. They are normally used to describe without prejudice, but often carry a slightly favorable connotation. The satirist changes the emotional impact of the word by teasing out a new and contrasting connotation which in effect re-defines the word and makes the thing it applies to blameworthy. Swift does this frequently. In *An Introduction to the Following Treatise,* for instance, "polite" comes to stand for emptiness, pretentiousness, vapidity. Charles Churchill, in *The Prophesy of Famine,* refers to the Scottish "invasion" of England:

> *Thence* simple bards, by simple prudence taught,
> To this *wise* town by simple patrons brought,
> In simple manner utter simple lays,
> And take, with simple pensions, simple praise.[47]

"Simple", which was frequently used with a favorable connotation in pastoral poetry, and without a pejorative connotation in general writing, has come to stand for something quite different; "self-seeking" is perhaps as close in a phrase as one can get. When a hundred-odd lines later he refers to "Ossian" as the *"sublimest, simplest* Bard of all", the new definition of the word is powerful enough not only to stigmatize Mac-Pherson, but to suggest an unfavorable connotation for "sublimest" as well. The narrator in *The Late George Apley* observes:

In the democracy of this [the Apley] family there was no barrier of age, and so the children were led into the drawing-room of a Sunday afternoon, where, after shaking hands and exchanging remarks with whoever might be present, they were placed in a silent row upon the sofa, obeying the maxim that "children should be seen and not heard."[48]

"Democracy" here seems to be roughly the equivalent of old-fashioned authoritarianism.

A third group consists of words which normally have a quite favorable denotation and connotation but in a given satire have been re-defined so drastically that a favorable connotation becomes an unfavorable one or the word may even reverse its meaning. The most familiar example is Mark Antony's speech in the Forum in *Julius Caesar.* "Honorable" is re-defined within the space of twenty or twenty-five lines until it

[47] *Poetical Works,* p. 198.
[48] John P. Marquand, *The Late George Apley: A Novel in the Form of a Memoir* (Boston, 1938), p. 33.

comes to have a meaning directly contrary to its normal one. Defoe uses the same tactic in *The Shortest Way with the Dissenters*. The way his persona uses "Charity" and "Mercy" gives the words a new and sinister meaning. In *Catch-22* a character called Nately announces that he is in love with an Italian girl and intends to marry her. His friend Aarfy receives the news with incredulous laughter:

"Married?" Aarfy's indulgent merriment swelled tremendously. "Ho, ho, ho ho, ho! Now you're really talking stupid. Why, you're not even old enough to know what true love is."

Aarfy was an authority on the subject of true love because he had already fallen truly in love with Nately's father and with the prospect of working for him after the war in some executive capacity as a reward for befriending Nately.[49]

No modern satirist has used re-definition more incisively than George Orwell. In *Animal Farm* the shattered hopes of the ordinary animals are epitomized by the change of the revolutionary slogan from "All Animals are Equal" to "ALL ANIMALS ARE EQUAL BUT SOME ANIMALS ARE MORE EQUAL THAN OTHERS". In *1984* Newspeak has been designated by the State "not only to provide a medium of expression for the world-view and mental habits proper to the devotees of Ingsoc [English Socialism], but to make all other modes of thought impossible".[50] The official Party slogans emblazoned on the Ministry of Truth are "WAR IS PEACE", "FREEDOM IS SLAVERY", "IGNORANCE IS STRENGTH". The final words of the satire distill the perversion of human values in the state of the future. Winston Smith has been beaten and tortured until only the husk of a human being remains. He sits in a cafe staring up at a portrait of Big Brother.

He gazed up at the enormous face. Forty years it had taken him to learn what kind of smile was hidden beneath the dark mustache. O cruel, needless misunderstanding! O stubborn, self-willed exile from the loving breast! Two gin-scented tears trickled down the sides of his nose. But it was all right, everything was all right, the struggle was finished. He had won the victory over himself. He loved Big Brother.[51]

In the re-defined meaning of "love" the whole, shattering point of the book is implicit.

As the examples I have cited above will suggest, the writer of satire appears to use re-definition in several different ways. First, the re-defini-

---

[49] Joseph Heller, *Catch-22* (New York, 1962), p. 296.
[50] Signet Classics (New York, 1962), p. 246.
[51] *1984*, p. 245.

tion may be used by the speaker in a satire as a matter of conscious
verbal irony. When the word is applied to the object of the satire the
usual meaning contrasts with the meaning the speaker has given it. The
effect is to contrast appearance with what he insinuates is reality. Thus
Antony's "honorable", in context is re-defined to mean something like
"dishonorable" and the speaker in *The Prophesy of Famine* uses
"simple" to mean "self-seeking". Secondly, re-definition may be used
to insinuate blame upon a character or persona who accepts and uses
a definition the reader recognizes is incomplete, mistaken, or morally
wrong. The reader blames Joseph Heller's Aarfy because his definition
of "true love" is askew. He blames the persona in *The Shortest Way
with the Dissenters,* the persona in *Introduction to the Following Treatise,* the leaders of the animals in *Animal Farm,* and the leaders of the
State in *1984.* The way they have re-defined words makes clear their
moral blindness or corruption. Finally, re-definition may work in still
more complex ways. At the end of *1984* Winston Smith "loves" Big
Brother. Yet his acceptance of love in this sense hardly insinuates his
own moral failing, for he has accepted this definition of love only after
being tried beyond the limits of human endurance. His acceptance is
an indictment of the corruption of values in the State, and perhaps
beyond this, of the social and human weaknesses which have led to the
world of *1984.*

   In all of these examples the contrast appears to be central to the
ɪatiric effect. The audience is aware of the "normal" meaning of the
re-defined word and, being aware, must contrast norm with deviation.
The contrast then insinuates a satiric meaning.

3. *Allusion and Echoing*

Another common satiric tactic is the establishment of relationships
between the satire and something outside the satire by alluding, or echo-
ing. A pattern of course may do this, but patterns not only allude, they
suggest a kind of structure or a kind of character. The allusions and
echoes I refer to here are essentially brief references which trigger the
reader's recollection of something else – very frequently a literary work
– and which insinuate blame by recalling the world outside the satire.

   The effect of the allusion may be to suggest one of two things. First,
it may recall a world outside the satire whose values are sounder, or
morally more praiseworthy than those in the satire. The contrast between
the two then insinuates blame. But the reverse may also happen. The

allusion may remind the audience of a world whose values are blameworthy. The insinuation in this case is that the values in the satire and
the values in the other world are alike. This second kind of allusion
works, in effect, to associate and might well have been discussed above
under "Association". However, since most allusions seem to set up an
implied contrast, it seems natural to include them here.

Neither the length of the allusion nor an exact echo of an original is
crucial. A single suggestive word is enough if it triggers the appropriate
recollection. A mere echo of Biblical phraseology is often enough for
Chaucer, Skelton and the Medieval satirists, Dryden, or Pope, to set up
the implied contrast. The Bible is by all odds the favorite source of satiric
allusions, for not only is it the best-known work in the English-speaking
world, but its turns of phrase are often distinctive enough to be recognizable even if a specific passage is not. Though its specific moral norms
vary from section to section, the Bible is inextricably associated with
morality and certain Christian virtues. The most fleeting allusion can
remind the reader of them.

The range of allusions which satirists have used is so vast and the
sources of them so multifarious that I shall not attempt to deal with
them comprehensively. However, a look at such an allusion in its context will suggest how most of them work. In Evelyn Waugh's *Decline
and Fall* Professor Otto Silenus, a modern architect, muses upon the
plan of a house he is building for Margot Beste-Chetwynde.

'I suppose there ought to be a staircase,' he said gloomily. 'Why can't the
creatures stay in one place? Up and down, in and out, round and round!
Why can't they sit still and work? Do dynamos require staircases? Do
monkeys require houses? What an immature, self-destructive antiquated
mischief is man! How obscure and gross his prancing and chattering on
his little stage of evolution! How loathsome and beyond words boring all
the thoughts and self-approval of this biological by-product! this half-
formed, ill-conditioned body! this erratic, maladjusted mechanism of his
soul: on one side the harmonious instincts and balanced responses of the
animal, on the other the inflexible purpose of the engine, and between
them man, equally alien from the *being* of Nature and the *doing* of the
machine, the vile *becoming*!"[52]

The passage of course echoes Hamlet's lyrical outburst: "What a
piece of work is a man! how noble in reason! how infinite in faculties!
in form and moving how express and admirable!"[53] The passages do
not suggest a complete contrast, for Hamlet's disgust with the way men

[52] *Decline and Fall*, pp. 120-121.
[53] II, ii, 316 ff.

act leads him to exclaim "Man delights not me – no, nor woman neither . . . ." This is superficially similar to Silenus' disgust with the human race. But these apparent similarities only serve to point up the vital contrast between Silenus' modern view and the Renaissance view of what man is. Hamlet's outburst is clearly a personal reaction. The world APPEARS foul and pestilent to him, and he can take no pleasure in human society, yet man IS a wondrous piece of work. There is no such idealistic conception of man beyond Professor Silenus' diatribe; man has neither the animal's harmonious adjustment to the world nor the machine's perfect adaptation to purpose. In this contrast between two views of man, a contrast which "works" very much like the contrast between the heroic world of the epic and the petty world of a mock-heroic poem, lies a good part of the effect of the satire.

While literary allusions or echoes are most frequent, almost any sort of reference may serve to suggest an insinuating contrast. Chaucer alludes to St. Maurus in his portrait of the Monk, Joyce to Parnell in "Ivy Day in the Committee Room". The effect in each case is roughly the same. St. Maurus suggests a standard of religious dedication which contrasts with the Monk's. Parnell, whatever his defects, had towering virtues; the contrast between him and the scrabbling, mean-spirited politicians of a latter-day Dublin is enough to insinuate Joyce's point.[54]

4. *Shifts in Perspective*

Another group of contrasts might be called contrasts or shifts in perspective, for they depend upon a shift in focus for their effect. The shift may, for example, demonstrate for the reader, or remind him, that a situation which appears innocuous from one point of view is blameworthy from another. Thus Evelyn Waugh reminds the readers of *Vile Bodies* to what estate the bearers of distinguished names have fallen in the Mayfair of the 1920's and 1930's:

[54] The allusion is often a book-title or chapter heading – *e.g.*, Huxley's *Brave New World* and *Antic Hay* ("My men, like satyrs grazing on the lawns/Shall with their goat feet dance an antic hay", Christopher Marlowe, *Edward II*); or Waugh's *Decline and Fall*, an echo of the title of Gibbon's great history. "Du Côté de Chez Beaver", a chapter title from *A Handful of Dust*, echoes Proust. When the allusion heads a whole section of a novel, or is its title, the effect of course is to put the whole work, or a large part of it, in a perspective which might not be obvious from allusions or references in the text proper. The echo of Gibbon in *Decline and Fall*, for instance, suggests a historical perspective, a moral evaluation, and an analogy between Rome and London that is suggested by nothing else in Waugh's text.

At Archie Schwert's party the fifteenth Marquess of Vanburgh, Earl Vanburgh de Brendon, Baron Brendon, Lord of the Five Isles and Hereditary Grand Falconer to the Kingdom of Connaught, said to the eighth Earl of Balcairn, Viscount Erdinge, Baron Cairn of Balcairn, Red Knight of Lancaster, Count of the Holy Roman Empire and Chenonceaux Herald to the Duchy of Aquitaine, 'Hullo,' he said. 'Isn't this a repulsive party? What are you going to say about it?' for they were both of them, as it happened, gossip writers for the daily papers.[55]

Or, in *Gulliver's Travels,* the Emperor of Lilliput is called

Golbasto Momaren Evlame Gurdilo Shefin Mully Ully Gue, most Mighty Emperor of *Lilliput*, Delight and Terror of the Universe, whose Dominions extend five thousand Blustrugs, (about twelve Miles in Circumference) . . .[56].

The straight-faced notation of the actual size of Lilliput immediately reminds us of the true size of his empire and restores a perspective which the reader may have been in danger of losing.

The shift in focus may have the effect of "plugging-into" a different world another contrasting set of moral values, the satiric point being insinuated simply by the contrast. In the opening lines of Henry Reed's *Naming of Parts* the shift is from the military world to the world of nature, its antithesis:

> Today we have naming of parts. Yesterday,
> We had daily cleaning. And tomorrow morning,
> We shall have what to do after firing. But today,
> Today we have naming of parts. Japonica
> Glistens like coral in all of the neighboring gardens,
>   And today we have naming of parts.[57]

In *Joseph Andrews,* Joseph is beaten by thieves, stripped naked, and left in a ditch beside the road. His groans are heard by the postilion of a stage-coach. It stops and after some debate its passengers agree to allow Joseph to enter. Modesty impels him to refuse until he is furnished with something to cover his nakedness.

Though there were several great-coats about the coach, it was not easy to get over this difficulty which Joseph had started. The two gentlemen complained they were cold, and could not spare a rag; the man of wit saying with a laugh, that charity began at home; and the coachman, who had two great-coats spread under him, refused to lend either, lest they should be made bloody: the lady's footman desired to be excused for the

[55] (Harmondsworth, Middlesex, 1951), p. 50.
[56] *Prose Works*, XI (1959), p. 43.
[57] *F. T. Palgrave's The Golden Treasury*, revised by Oscar Williams, Mentor Edition (New York, 1961), p. 550.

same reason, which the lady herself, notwithstanding her abhorrence of a naked man, approved: and it is more than probable poor Joseph, who obstinately adhered to his modest resolution, must have perished, unless the postilion (a lad who hath been since transported for robbing a hen-roost) had voluntarily stript off a great-coat, his only garment, at the same time swearing a great oath (for which he was rebuked by the passengers), "That he would rather ride in his shirt all his life, than suffer a fellow-creature to lie in so miserable a condition."[58]

The shift here is of course from the present scene to the future. Fielding's apparently casual interjection that the charitable postilion has been transported for a trivial offense cuts several ways. It insinuates a reflection upon the contemporary legal code. It is an implied commentary upon moralistic fiction in which virtue IS rewarded. And since the charitable postilion has been transported and we can't imagine any of the others who refuse to help Joseph meeting a similar fate, the interjection suggests a sardonic view of rewards for virtue and punishments for vice in the world in which Joseph Andrews and his friends live.

The lines which open Canto III of *The Rape of the Lock* illustrate the same tactic in a still more complex way.

> Close by those Meads for ever crown'd with Flow'rs,
> Where *Thames* with Pride surveys his rising Tow'rs.
> There stands a Structure of Majestick Frame,
> Which from the neighb'ring *Hampton* takes its Name.
> Here *Britain's* Statesmen oft the Fall foredoom
> Of Foreign Tyrants, and of Nymphs at home;
> Here Thou, Great *Anna*! whom three Realms obey,
> Dost sometimes Counsel take – and sometimes *Tea*.
>   Hither the Heroes and the Nymphs resort,
> To taste awhile the Pleasures of a Court;
> In various Talk th' instructive hours they past,
> Who gave the *Ball*, or paid the *Visit* last:
> One speaks the Glory of the *British Queen,*
> And one describes a charming *Indian Screen*;
> A third interprets Motions, Looks, and Eyes;
> At ev'ry Word a Reputation dies.
> *Snuff*, or the *Fan*, supply each Pause of Chat,
> With singing, laughing, ogling, and all that.
>   Mean while declining from the Noon of Day,
> The Sun obliquely shoots his burning Ray;
> The hungry Judges soon the Sentence sign,
> And Wretches hang that Jury-men may Dine;
> The Merchant from th'*Exchange* returns in Peace,
> And the long Labours of the *Toilette* cease –
> *Belinda* now, whom Thirst of Fame invites,

---

[58] *Joseph Andrews*, pp. 47-48.

Burns to encounter two adventrous Knights,
At *Ombre* singly to decide their Doom;
And swells her Breast with Conquests yet to come.

Pope's lines shift the focus from the world of the beau monde and the world of airy spirits in Canto II to the "real" world outside, the world of the Court, of the law courts, of business. The shifts to the larger and more serious worlds outside put Belinda's world in perspective. They do more than this of course, for these references are qualified. Their subject's pretences to seriousness, grandeur, or morality are modified by other shifts in focus. The "Majestick Frame" of Hampton Court is conjured up not only as a backdrop for Belinda and her friends, but for British statesmen who are part of the more serious world which is being contrasted with Belinda's. They are also the butt of the insinuation inherent in the shift of focus in "the Fall foredoom/ Of Foreign Tyrants, and of Nymphs at home". The theological overtones of "Fall" emphasize the moral confusion touched upon more than once in the poem. The grandeur of the monarchy is invoked – "*Great* Anna!" – then undercut by the mocking "whom three Realms obey" (the fiction that the English crown ruled France as well as Ireland and the United Kingdom was still maintained), then re-established again – "Dost sometimes Counsel take" – before the reference to the tea-table reminds us of the rather commonplace woman who occupied the throne. The serious office of the judge is suggested only to be undercut by the narrator's reference to the judges' haste to reach the dinner table. The merchant's labors at the Exchange, like the lady's at the toilet-table, are only preparations for more serious business in the evening. The constant shifts magnify only to diminish. The whole passage is a constantly shifting network of insinuation which at one moment implies a point of view from which to observe the fashionable world, then next reminds us that the larger world which envelopes Belinda's is itself pretentious or morally equivocal.

Magnification and diminution – what Pope called "magnifying" and "diminishing" – are worth mentioning in connection with shifts in perspective. The general method is simply to exploit a difference in size, and to make the difference seem blameworthy. Magnifying the object of the satire makes its faults seem larger, diminishing it makes it seem more petty or absurd. Perhaps the simplest forms involve a contrast in physical size. The contrast between Gulliver and the Lilliputians makes the pride of such insignificant creatures seem ludicrous, as the reverse contrast between Gulliver and the Brobdingnagians makes

Gulliver, in his turn, seem petty. Alice's changes in size in *Alice in Wonderland* change the perspective of the reader toward the people and the animals she meets later. The effects of some satiric animal fables turn upon the contrast in size, since the animals may be considerably smaller or considerably larger than human beings. Transferring human types and patterns of conduct to the animal world alters the perspective and, like any change in perspective, provides a point of view which may be exploited for satiric purposes. However, contrasts based upon differences in physical size are relatively rare. Most magnifying and diminishing involves not physical, but figurative contrasts in size and these may be achieved by using, or combining, a wide variety of tactics.

5. Contrasts between Expectation and "Reality"

Frequently, magnification precedes diminution; the balloon is blown up as far as it will go before the needle is inserted. Milton is using a standard satiric tactic in *Paradise Lost* when he inflates Satan to grandiose size in the early part of the poem before diminishing him in the scenes in Hell in which Satan becomes a serpent and is hissed at by the assembled fallen angels. Chaucer's Prioress is so charitable and so compassionate that she would weep if she saw a mouse caught in a trap. In *The Battle of the Books* the magnificently mounted Virgil, clad in shining armor "compleatly fitted to his Body" meets Dryden wearing a "Helmet ... nine times too large for the Head ... like a Mouse under a Canopy of State".[59] Magnifying and diminishing are of course basic to much satiric character portrayal. They underlie many of the satiric as well as comic effects in *Hudibras*, and in Fielding's and Dickens' novels. They are used to undercut "experts", like the explorer Dr. Messinger in *A Handful of Dust*, a kind of undercutting frequent in the works of Evelyn Waugh.

Magnifying followed by diminishing is often anti-climactic and anti-climax too may be used as a satiric tactic. Usually the writer of the satire builds to a climax then gives the reader what is perhaps not a genuine anti-climax, but an unexpected climax which has the effect of undercutting what has preceded, throwing it into an unexpected, blameworthy perspective. The following are typical, brief examples:

The abbey of Rubygill stood in a picturesque valley, at a little distance from the boundary of Sherwood Forest, in a spot which seemed adapted

[59] *Prose Works*, I (1957), 157.

by nature to be the retreat of monastic mortification, being on the banks of a fine trout-stream, and in the midst of woodland coverts, abounding with excellent game.[60]

(Peacock, *Maid Marian*)

Martin Chuzzlewit has been examining a copy of the New York *Rowdy Journal,* and the colonel asks him what he thinks of it:

'Why, it's horribly personal,' said Martin.

The colonel seemed much flattered by this remark; and said he hoped it was.

'We are independent here, sir,' said Mr. Jefferson Brick. 'We do as we like.'

'If I may judge from this specimen,' returned Martin, 'there must be a few thousands here, rather the reverse of independent, who do as they don't like.'

'Well! They yield to the mighty mind of the Popular Instructor, sir,' said the colonel. 'They rile up, sometimes; but in general we have a hold upon our citizens, both in public and in private life, which is as much one of the ennobling institutions of our happy country as –'.

'As nigger slavery itself,' suggested Mr. Brick.

'En – tirely so,' remarked the colonel.[61]

I have a black dog with cheeks of tan. Her number is 11032. It is an old number. I shall renew it when I get time. The analysis of her prepared food is guaranteed and is Case Number 1312. The ingredients are: Cereal Flaked feeds (from Corn, Rice, Bran, and Wheat), Meat Meal, Fish Liver and Glandular Meal, Soybean Oil Meal, Wheat Bran, Corn Germ Meal, 5% Kel-Concentrate [containing Dried Skim Milk, Dehydrated Cheese, Vitamin B_1 (Thiamin), Flavin Concentrate, Carotene, Yeast, Vitamin A and D Feeding Oil (containing 3,000 U.S.P. units Vitamin A and 400 U.S.P. units Vitamin D per gram), Diastase (Enzyme), Wheat Germ Meal, Rice Polish Extract], 1½% Calcium Carbonate, .00037% Potassium Iodide, and ¼% Salt. She prefers offal.[62]

(E. B. White, "About Myself")

Another common form of satiric anti-climax is to portray a character whose ideal is confounded with "reality". Nathanael West's Lemuel Pitkin and his friend Betty Phrail are standing in the street when a policeman who had been watching them approaches.

"Get along, you rats," he said gruffly.

"I resent your talking that way to a lady," said Lem indignantly.

"What's that?" asked the officer lifting his club.

[60] *The Novels of Thomas Love Peacock,* p. 445.
[61] *The Works of Charles Dickens,* The National Library Edition De Luxe (New York, n.d.), XIV, 361-362.
[62] *The Second Tree from the Corner,* pp. 74-75.

"We are both citizens of this country and you have no right to treat us in this manner," went on Lem fearlessly.

The patrolman was just about to bring his truncheon down on the lad's skull, when Betty interfered and dragged him away.[63]

Byron's Don Juan, walking on the summit of Shooter's Hill, muses about England:

> "Here are chaste wives, pure lives; here people pay
>   But what they please; and if that things be dear,
> 'Tis only that they love to throw away
>   Their cash, to show how much they have a year.
> Here laws are all inviolate; none lay
>   Traps for the traveller; every highway's clear;
> Here" – he was interrupted by a knife,
> With – "Damn your eyes! your money or your life!" –[64]

In the tenth chapter of Part III of *Gulliver's Travels,* Gulliver first hears of the immortal Struldbrugs and bursts into rapturous praise of the happiness of those

who being born exempt from that universal Calamity of human Nature, have their Minds free and disingaged, without the Weight and Depression of Spirits caused by the continual Apprehension of Death.[65]

He wonders why the ruler of the country has not provided himself with Struldbrug counselors, and announces himself ready to pass his life in their company if they would please to admit him. He is asked how he would have conducted his life had he been born a Struldbrug and is led on to outline an existence devoted to the acquisition of wisdom and the defense of morality. Then the awful truth about the Struldbrugs is revealed – although life continues, their faculties decay, and the Struldbrugs long for nothing more than death.

In all three of these examples part of the effect of the contrast between what the character expects, or what ideally should be, and things as they actually are, is to satirize the character himself. He is naive, a gull. But in each case the satire goes beyond mere exposure of his innocence. Insofar as Pitkin, Juan, and Gulliver all expect the ideal and are confounded by reality they satirize a general human failing. The likeness ends here, however. Pitkin's discomfiture reveals a blameworthy gap between the spirit of the law and the way it is carried out in prac-

---

[63]   *A Cool Million,* in *The Complete Works of Nathanael West,* p. 214.

[64]   In *Don Juan and Other Satirical Poems,* ed. Louis I. Bredvold (New York 1935), p. 545.

[65]   *Prose Works,* XI (1959), 208.

tice. Juan's undercuts a typically English idealization of English people and society. Gulliver's satirizes the all-too-human tendency to assume that physical immortality would be an unmixed blessing.

6. *Contrasts Between Praise and Blame*

Earlier I mentioned contrasts between two different channels of satire — the alternation between overstatement and insinuation, which is characteristic of mixed satire, and the interjection of a direct authorial comment, which sometimes initiates the satiric shock by alerting the reader to insinuation and begins the process of enlisting his cooperation. I mentioned also inverted praise, which is the manner of proceeding in mock panegyrics like Churchill's *Dedication to the Sermons* and the opening section of Pope's *To Augustus*. All of these differ from another sort of contrast, namely, the contrast between blame and genuine praise — that is, straightforward praise for actions and qualities that seem genuinely praiseworthy. One effect of contrasting praise and blame is simply to deepen the dye of the objects of the satire by contrasting them with others — frequently others with similar backgrounds and opportunities — who have acted in a less blameworthy manner. This sort of contrast is one of the tactics used in Churchill's *The Rosciad,* Swift's *The Battle of the Books*, and *Absalom and Achitophel*. This latter, particularly, is a skillfully adjusted mixture of praise and blame — each necessary to the other's full effect.

The praise and blame may be assigned to individual figures — each appearing relatively black or white — but more subtle and effective is the tactic of praising the object of the satire before, or as part of, a satiric thrust. The praise may be for minor or irrelevant virtues, or even for genuinely great or noble ones. Thus Dryden praises Shaftesbury's abilities as a judge, and Byron, George the Third's domestic and bucolic virtues. Pope's portrait of Atticus begins by praising

> . . . One whose fires
> True Genius kindles, and fair Fame inspires,
> Blest with each Talent and each Art to please,
> And born to write, converse, and live with ease:[66]

Only then does he launch into the famous attack.

Lines like these strengthen the satire in more than one way. They throw the reader somewhat off guard so that the acid which follows has

[66] *Poems*, 2nd ed, IV, 109-110, ll. 193-196.

a greater effect. They suggest the satirist's "fairness", and thus lend authority to the denunciation which follows. Perhaps most important, they make it clear that Atticus had great abilities but has made poor use of them; and the waste or perversion of great abilities always seems more blameworthy than the failure to possess them. All of these things contribute to the satiric effect. Praise, in satire, is usually not there for its own sake. It is there to contrast with blame, and thus lend blame a sharper cutting edge.

7. Contrasts Involving Character and Scene

Contrasts between praise and blame are inseparable from – in fact in some cases hardly distinguishable from – contrasts between characters and contrasts between scenes. The contrast may be between a relatively sensible or praiseworthy character and various others who are being satirized (such as the contrast between Pope himself and Atticus and Bufo and Sporus in the *Epistle to Dr. Arbuthnot*, or between Cornelius and his more reasonable brother in *Martinus Scriblerus*, or Mark Rampion and the other characters in *Point Counter Point*, or between Mr. Hilary and the others in *Nightmare Abbey*). In satires like these the sensible character suggests, or embodies a norm and the others appear as deviants measured by referring to this norm. The contrast may be between an ingénu and the blameworthy people he meets (Huck Finn in some of the episodes of *Huckleberry Finn*, Paul Pennyfeather in *Decline and Fall*, for example). The ingénu does not so much embody a norm as fail to understand the mores of the society in which he finds himself. His innocence suggests another, simpler, scale of values out-side the satire and these values throw those of the other characters into sharp relief. The contrast may also be between characters who are being satirized with different degrees of intensity, or for somewhat different reasons. The norm which emerges – if it can be said to "emerge" at all – is one which the audience must attempt to arrive at by finding a common center from which blameworthy deviations can be measured. In Peter de Vries' *The Mackerel Plaza*, for example, the norm must be inferred by assaying the religious views not only of Reverend Mackerel himself, but of his evangelical parishioners, the young minister who replaces him, and so on. In Evelyn Waugh's *A Handful of Dust* a norm is represented neither by Tony Last, who lives in a Victorian Gothic world and is incapable of coping with the modern one, nor by the heartless Brenda and her friends. We are left to infer the norm.

Contrasts between scenes often work in conjunction with contrasts between characters and the same general comments apply. In satiric novels and short stories, particularly, the satiric point is often implicit in a contrast between two juxtaposed scenes. The first chapters of *Brave New World* consist largely of such contrasted scenes and the tactic is basic to the satire of satiric novelists such as Huxley, Waugh, Sinclair Lewis, and the John dos Passos of *U.S.A.* However, the long, intricate fabric of *The Canterbury Tales* is perhaps the best example in English of the ways in which character may be contrasted with character and scene with scene to suggest meanings which neither character nor scene would have in isolation. Throughout the *Tales* the audience is constantly made aware of what Charles Muscatine calls Chaucer's "tireless capacity for definition and comparison".[67] These comparisons – and we might add, contrasts – are often pointed enough to heighten effects which are clearly satiric even without them, but sometimes a juxtaposition seems to point to a satiric effect which we might otherwise miss or fail to appreciate fully.

In "The General Prologue" for example, few readers are likely to miss the satire implicit in the portraits of the Monk and the Friar, but in both cases the satire is heightened by the portrait of the Parson. The Parson represents an ideal, and the very fact that an ideal is portrayed sharpens the satire on the other ecclesiastics. Once the ideal has been established, it may be exploited most economically to imply, or heighten, a satiric effect. At the end of *The Pardoner's Tale* the Pardoner and the Host quarrel and exchange the most scurrilous sort of insults. The quarrel is smoothed over by the Knight. The fact that the Knight smoothes over the quarrel is natural enough, for he is the most respected of the pilgrims who are not in holy orders. The fact that he is introduced at this point in the narrative deepens and enriches the satire on the Pardoner, for the very mention of the Knight's name evokes again the nobility of the idealized courtly world which the Knight represents and contrasts his magnanimity with the depravity of the money-hungry Pardoner thereby throwing the Pardoner's world into sharp relief.

The individual tales interact upon one another, also, and the very fact of this interaction sometimes suggests, or sharpens a satiric point. *The Miller's Tale* immediately follows *The Knight's Tale* and, to some degree, parodies it. The three courtly lovers have their counterparts in Alisoun, Nicholas, and Absalom; there are realistic portraits of the two

---

[67] *Chaucer and the French Tradition: A Study in Style and Meaning* (Berkeley and Los Angeles, 1957), p. 223.

clerks, and of Alisoun, as there are courtly ones of Palamon, Arcite, and of Emilye. The turning of the wheel of fortune in the courtly tale suggests that the raising and abrupt descent of the tub in the "realistic" *Miller's Tale* may be intended as parody, too.

The effect of the parody is to imply a norm which is not the norm of either tale, but lies somewhere between. *The Knight's Tale* implies a criticism of the standards of the everyday world; *The Miller's Tale* implies a criticism of the courtly conventions. Somewhere between them lies another norm. Thus the tales interact upon one another and the interaction itself implies a meaning which is not implicit in either alone.

8. *Contrasts Between Satire and Non-satire*

A final group of contrasts includes many of the points I have already mentioned, yet seems to need an additional brief discussion. This is the contrast between satiric and non-satiric passages within the same work. Contrasts of this sort work in several ways. The contrast may of course intensify the effect of both the satiric and non-satiric passages, as it frequently does in Byron. In *Beppo* he moves with the greatest ease from gravity to mockery, and in *Don Juan* sentiment and ridicule, sublimity and farce succeed each other with bewildering rapidity. In the first canto, mockery of institutions, cynicism, light raillery, pungent lampooning, and knockabout farce are succeeded by the genuine sentiment of Julia's farewell letter to Juan. It begins:

> "They tell me 'tis decided; you depart:
>   'Tis wise – 'tis well, but not the less a pain;
> I have no further claim on your young heart,
>   Mine is the victim, and would be again;
> To love too much has been the only art
>   I used; – I write in haste, and if a stain
> Be on this sheet, 'tis not what it appears;
> My eyeballs burn and throb, but have no tears."[68]

Julia's feeling is not being mocked – the pathos of the letter is un-alloyed by ridicule. The contrast is arresting and it heightens the effect of both the satire and the sentiment.

The contrasts may also, by the interaction of the satiric and non-satiric passages, help to define the meaning of the work as a whole, as they do in novels which have clearly satiric sections, yet resist any easy

[68] *Don Juan and Other Satirical Poems*, ed. Louis I. Bredvold (New York, 1935), p. 217.

classification as "satires". Many of Dickens' and Jane Austen's novels fall into this category, as do modern novels like *Zuleika Dobson, Catch-22,* and Bernard Malamud's *The Natural.* This sort of contrast is clearest in works like *The Pickwick Papers* and *The Great Gatsby* which begin as satires, then shift. The early chapters of the latter, for instance, are clearly satiric. Gatsby is a vulgar, ostentatious, ignorant *parvenu* who gives fantastic parties for groups of casually assembled guests. Gatsby and the whole world which surrounds him seem to be patterned, partly at least, upon the "Dinner with Trimalchio" sequence in Petronius' *The Satyricon,* and Gatsby has some clear affinities with Trimalchio himself. Both wear vulgar, incongruous clothing, both give expensive, ostentatious gifts, both are interrupted at their parties by business deals, both have expensive libraries assembled for show rather than use. Trimalchio is ludicrously confused about mythology and history and geography – he places Hannibal at the sack of Troy and confuses Cassandra with Medea. This sort of grand confusion suggests Gatsby's equally heroic lapse. When Nick Carraway, the narrator of the novel, asks Gatsby what part of the Middle West his parents come from, Gatsby replies "San Francisco". In *The Great Gatsby,* however, the satire is replaced as the novel continues by a much more sympathetic portrait of the central figure. Nick Carraway comes to see Gatsby as the perfection of a kind of romantic idealism which he learns to admire. Most readers, too, accept Nick's evaluation and come to accept Gatsby, in some favorable sense of the word, as "great". In short, what begins as satire ends as romantic novel. Though the total effect of the novel is non-satiric, the satire plays an important part, for the shift from satire to non-satire parallels Nick's growing understanding of Gatsby, and doubtless ours, too. The progression in other words is from an outer satiric view to an inner, much more compassionate one and each is necessary to the total effect of the novel.[69]

[69] One might argue that the shift from satire suggests a fundamental uncertainty in Fitzgerald's view of Gatsby, a suggestion which is supported by Fitzgerald's own statement in a letter to John Peale Bishop that the portrait of Gatsby was "blurred and patchy. I never at any one time saw him clear myself – for he started out as one man I knew and then changed into myself. . . ." (*The Crack-Up,* New York, 1945, 271). Yet what Fitzgerald admits is a fault in conception works out remarkably well in practice. I discussed the matter – rather wrong-headedly, I now think – in "In Incomplete Amalgam: The Tone of 'The Great Gatsby' " (*The English Record,* XIV [October, 1963], 26-31), an essay upon which part of the above is based.

VII

CONCLUSION

In the "Introduction", I referred to Wellek and Warren's useful criteria for distinguishing a genre. It will be helpful to recall them:

Genre should be conceived, we think, as a grouping of literary works based, theoretically, upon both outer form (specific meter or structure) and also upon inner form (attitude, tone, purpose – more crudely, subject and audience). The ostensible basis may be one or the other ... but the critical problem will then be to find the *other* dimension, to complete the diagram.

We can carry the argument begun in the "Introduction" to a conclusion now by drawing together the points made at some length above. Satire is a genre characterized by its aggressive purpose (*i.e.*, its inner form), and by certain insinuating devices or, as I have chosen to call them, tactics (the outer form). A "satire" then is an aggressive work which, in its most typical form, shocks its audience into awareness that it is not to be read literally, and, this awareness established, insinuates the blame of the object of the satire by creating a persona, by playing pattern against the content of the satire, or by any of the various other tactics discussed in Chapter VI. As a matter of convenience I have discussed these tactics in relative isolation, but they seem invariably to be used in conjunction with one another – though of course not all are used in every satire.

Jonathan Swift's *A Modest Proposal* is a convenient illustration of the way tactics are used in combination because it uses a variety of tactics in a relatively short space, and is so familiar that I need not preface an analysis with an extensive summary. The context in which the reader of 1729 would have read the essay, though not strictly a "tactic", is important. It included knowledge of the recent famine in Ireland, the general poverty and wretchedness of the lower classes, the exactions and oppressions of the landlords and politicians, both Irish and English, previous schemes which had been proposed to ameliorate

conditions in Ireland, and a widely held economic maxim of the time –
that people were the "riches" of a country.[1] Not every reader would
have known all of these things, but it seems reasonable to assume that
most readers would have known most of them. Some knowledge of
context is the necessary background against which the tactics operate.

The pattern of *A Modest Proposal* is that of a tract and as far as the
actual pattern itself is concerned is quite similar to other economic
tracts of the time.[2] Adopting the pattern of non-satiric works provides
a disguise for Swift's insinuation and helps prepare for the satiric shock.
It does more than this, of course. Since the pattern recalls certain other
economic tracts whose authors had argued that human beings were the
real wealth of a country, Swift's tract insinuates that there is at least one
nation whose poverty makes it an exception to the rule. Lest the point
be missed, he states it directly near the end of the tract: "I calculate my
Remedy *for this one individual Kingdom of Ireland* . . .". (116)[3]

The tract is apparently written in the first person by a Protestant
Irishman who professes a disinterested love of his country. This is the
persona of course. He is characterized in some detail and is clearly not
to be identified with Swift himself. The fact that he is a member of the
ruling class helps define the target of the satire. It is directed not against
a single individual, but the class he represents. The persona makes it
plain he knows the conditions in Ireland at first hand, and that he stands
to gain nothing personally from the scheme he proposes. Thus he
contrasts with other projectors whose schemes have been based upon a
cursory acquaintance with the situation, or who have been influenced
by selfish interests.[4] Both the pattern and the persona thus help to
insinuate blame upon others who have written about conditions in Ireland.

The persona begins by describing the contemporary scene in Ireland,
selecting and accentuating the one aspect of poverty and desperation of

[1] See Louis A. Landa, "*A Modest Proposal* and Populousness", *Modern Philology*,
XL (1942), 161-170.
[2] Herbert Davis, whose "Introduction" to *The Prose Works*, XII (1955), includes
a survey of non-satiric tracts on the Irish problem says, "it follows exactly the
shape and form of all these various proposals of one kind or another with very
specific details worked out, and with careful calculations of all the possible advantages and disadvantages of the scheme" (p. xx).
[3] *Prose Works*, XII. Landa discusses the point in detail. Page references throughout the chapter are to Volume XII of *Prose Works*.
[4] A point made by Ewald in *The Masks of Jonathan Swift*, pp. 164-165. I am
indebted to Ewald for some of the points made throughout this section.

the native Irish. The straightforwardness and plainness of the persona's style and the "reasonableness" of the scheme he proposes are the most important ingredients of the businesslike, matter-of-fact surface tone of the tract. It is in violent contrast with the actual emotions induced in the reader when he learns the real nature of the project. There is a contrast, too, between the humanity of the speaker, who is moved by the plight of the "innocent Babes", and the apparent cruelty of the scheme. Both contrasts are central to the effect. As conditions exist in Ireland, it is both reasonable and humane to argue that children should be eaten, for this is a happier prospect than the general wretchedness and misery which is the only other prospect they have.

The scheme the projector has conceived for the alleviation of the general distress is at first discussed in rather general terms and it is not until we are fairly well into the piece that its actual nature is disclosed. The shock comes of course in the line "I have been assured by a very knowing *American* of my acquaintance in *London*; that a young healthy Child, well nursed, is at a Year old, a most delicious, nourishing, and wholesome Food" (p. 111). At least this is the point at which the average reader would have been shocked. A more acute reader might have been put on his guard by earlier references to "a Child, *just dropt from its Dam*" (p. 110), or the persona's identification of himself as a "Projector", or several other references. But at whatever point the shock occurs, the effect is to force him to readjust the set with which he has been reading. He has been warned that the writer of the satire is insinuating something he is not saying directly. Having been fooled once, he does not want to be fooled again. He not only reads with greater attention, he cooperates more actively with the satirist, becoming a fuller participant in the satire. His increased alertness leads him through several stages of awareness. His first reaction may be that the projector is morally wrong; people should not eat people. Then he recognizes that what the projector says is ruthlessly logical. Finally he recognizes the truth of the situation; he sees the condition of Ireland in the perspective in which Swift wants him to see it, which could have been shown in no other way. As conditions are in Ireland, the projector is not only logically right, he is humane as well. When he observes "Cruelty . . . hath always been with me the strongest Objection against any Project," (113), he may be speaking the truth. His project is less cruel than the prospect which faces the Irish poor.

The style is lucid, straightforward, unadorned, as an example from the second page will suggest:

As to my own Part, having turned my Thoughts for many Years, upon
this important Subject, and maturely weighed the several *Schemes of other
Projectors*, I have always found them grosly mistaken in their Computation.
It is true a Child, *just dropt from its Dam*, may be supported by her Milk,
for a Solar Year with little other Nourishment; at most not above the Value
of two Shillings; which the Mother may certainly get, or the Value in
Scraps, by her lawful Occupation of *Begging*: And, it is exactly at one
Year old, that I propose to provide for them in such a Manner, as, instead
of being a Charge upon their *Parents*, or the *Parish*, or wanting *Food and
Raiment* for the rest of their lives; they shall, on the contrary, contribute
to the Feeding, and partly to the Cloathing, of many Thousands.

(p. 110)

The persona frequently uses terminology drawn from animal hus-
bandry to describe the Irish poor ("a Child . . *dropt from its Dam*",
"Breeders", "Carcase", and "fore or hind Quarters"), which has the
effect of equating animal and human and reinforcing the insinuation
of moral blindness. He links animals and humans by analogy. One of
the advantages of adopting his scheme, he suggests, is that "Men would
becomes as *fond* of their Wives, during the Time of their Pregnancy, as
they now are of their *Mares* in Foal, their *Cows* in Calf, or *Sows* when
they are ready to farrow; nor offer to beat or kick them, (as it is too
frequent a Practice) for fear of a Miscarriage" (p. 115). There is a
double insinuation here; first that Irishmen, under present conditions,
look upon children as less valuable than domestic animals, and second,
that they are so in dread of additional mouths to feed that they
frequently attempt to induce abortions by wife-beating.

The persona says "I have already computed the Charge of nursing
a Beggar's Child (in which List I reckon all *Cottagers, Labourers,* and
Four fifths of the *Farmers*) . . ." (p. 112). Here he is re-defining and
expanding the meaning of the word "Beggar" to include not only those
mendicants the reader would ordinarily include within the definition,
but virtually all the lower classes. The effect of the re-definition, of
course, is to intensify the impression of general poverty and degradation.
He speaks of the children of the poor "*wanting Food and Raiment*"
(p. 110). The phrase "Food and Raiment" is an echo of I Timothy 6:8
of the King James Bible, in which Paul writes a letter to Timothy and
speaks of the proper relationship of masters and servants, and of the
evils that spring from the love of money.[5] The application to Irish landlords and Irish tenants is obvious.

[5]   The passage itself is familiar enough, but even if the reader does not recognize
it, he is likely to respond to the general echo of Biblical phraseology.

The American referred to in the quotation above, and later the Chinese, are associated with the barbarous practice of cannibalism, and throughout the essay Irish landlords and fine gentlemen generally are associated with them, and thus with cannibalism, since the assumption is that they will welcome the scheme and enjoy the meat thus provided. Underlying the whole project is an allegorical idea based upon a "logical" extension of what is figuratively happening in Ireland. The oppressors of the Irish are in effect, if not in fact, EATING the poor.

The voice of the persona is interrupted in several places. At one of these places he says, "if the same Use were made of several plump young girls in this Town, who, without one single Groat to their Fortunes, cannot stir Abroad without a Chair, and appear at the *Play-house,* and *Assemblies* in foreign Fineries, which they will never pay for; the Kingdom would not be the worse" (p. 114). This seems to be Swift rather than the persona speaking. The shift might be called an artistic flaw – a loosening of Swift's control of his material – but it serves a tactical purpose nonetheless. It underscores his criticism of the luxuries and follies which have contributed to the present state of affairs, criticisms which he reverts to a little later in another direct passage, and the contrast between overstatement and the various forms of insinuation used throughout the piece helps to focus the reader's attention on the insinuation and to sharpen its effect.

These are the chief tactics Swift uses in *A Modest Proposal*. The examples I have given are not exhaustive, for some of the tactics are used more than once. A full explication would account for them all, but this brief listing will illustrate well enough how tactics work in combination. Three of the tactics are pervasive: pattern, shock, and persona. The pattern suggests a perspective – the perspective provided by contemporary economic tracts. Shock forces the reader into a realization that the discourse is not to be taken literally, and induces him to cooperate with the satirist. The use of the persona provides a medium which focuses the reader's attention upon conditions in Ireland as Swift wants them to be seen.

The other tactics are not so pervasive, but intensify and define particular points which contribute to the total effect of the essay. One of the important things they do is to make it clear which interpretation of two or more possible ones is the right one. In a passage I quoted above the persona says that Irishmen frequently beat or kick their wives. If the passage were considered in isolation, one might argue that it is simply a slur upon Irishmen for being cruel to their wives. In context, however, the insinuation that beatings which result in abortion are the result of economic conditions, not cruelty alone, seems unmistakable.

Obviously, no mere analysis of tactics will wholly explain a good indirect satire any more than an analysis of poetic devices will wholly explain a good poem. But an account of the tactics at work within the satire gives us at least a partial insight into the way the rich and complex effect of the satire is produced, a far more formidable effect than any direct statement about the appalling conditions in Ireland could achieve.

Thus far I have tried to distinguish the three channels in which English satire has traditionally flowed, and to isolate the tactics characteristic of the main channel, indirect satire. Of course these tactics are not found in indirect satire only; they are found, though less frequently, in other literary perspectives as well. Perhaps it will be useful to conclude, therefore, by drawing attention to the lines between indirect satire and the boundaries of other, related perspectives. These boundaries are hardly sharp lines of cleavage; there is a twilight zone between them in which it is unprofitable, if not absurd, to be too categorical. But the main areas may at least be sketched.

I have already referred to some of the terms which are frequently applied to satiric works, or works which lie close to the boundaries of satire. Lampoons, parodies, and high and low burlesques use combinations of the tactics we have been considering. The lampoon is simply a satire directed at an individual. It may be indirect, but most lampoons are direct or mixed satires. The parody is a form of literary criticism. If it is aggressive, we can claim it for satire, but it is perhaps worth noting that the tone of many parodies seems to be affectionately comic, rather than satiric, and that really savage literary criticism is usually not parody, but invective. Thus the parodies that belong to satire are usually only mildly aggressive and belong near the borders of satire and comedy. A low burlesque uses tactics whose effect is to reduce the stature of the object of the satire below its usual status. "Travesty" is often used as a synonym, though it may be used to refer to a special kind of low burlesque in which figures or themes which have appeared in serious, or classic, literature, are diminished. A high burlesque reverses the process; the effect of the tactics is to elevate the object of the satire above its usual status. "Mock-heroic", or "mock-epic", is sometimes used as a synonym for high burlesque; sometimes, too, it is used more narrowly to designate a high burlesque whose tactics effect an association of the object of the satire with the world of the heroic poem. Like the parody, the burlesque is only sometimes aggressive. When it is non-aggressive, it belongs to comedy rather than satire.

The exact line of demarcation between the satiric and the comic has always eluded precise definition. Are Evelyn Waugh's *Decline and Fall* and *Vile Bodies* comic or satiric novels? How satiric are Swift's *A Meditation on a Broom-stick* and Pope's *The Dignity, Use and Abuse of Glass-bottles?* Are the Wife of Bath and Sir John Falstaff creations of the comic or the satiric imagination? No answer will satisfy all critics in all periods, for the way in which the works are classified depends upon such variables as the historical context in which the work is read and the context which the individual reader brings to it.

The effect of many satiric tactics is to make the object of the satire amusing, and there is no doubt that laughter plays an important part in such satire. It is equally certain that laughter is not absolutely necessary to *all* satire, though many distinguished critics have argued the contrary. Few fully perceptive readers are likely to laugh at *The Shortest Way with the Dissenters,* much of Part IV of *Gulliver's Travels,* or *A Modest Proposal.* In fact, as Kenneth Tynan has pointed out, laughter may even undercut the effect the writer of certain kinds of satire hopes to achieve: "to the satirist . . . a sense of humour may . . . be an embarrassment, since the idea of disinterested laughter – laughter for its own sake, an end rather than a means – clearly subverts the premise on which his purposeful art is based. To the satirist, pure humour is a waste of valuable laughter."[6] Qualifiers like "light" and "bitter" which are frequently applied to satire, often seem to be used to suggest the amount of laughter the satire evokes. A light or playful satire is usually one which is amusing. Bitter satire, on the other hand, usually denotes satire which approaches the intensity and somberness of tragedy.

But the question of whether or not a satire evokes laughter is too subjective to be really illuminating. There is no doubt that it is witty, or that the indirect satirist embodies the conscious slyness which Louis Cazamian argues is a distinctive quality of the humorist.[7] In borderline cases three differing tendencies help to distinguish comedy from satire. 1) While both comedy and satire stress incongruity, the emphasis in

---

[6] *The [London] Observer Weekend Review,* January 13, 1963.
[7] See *The Development of English Humor* (Durham, North Carolina, 1952), *passim.*

satire is not upon the incongruity itself, but upon the blameworthiness of one of the incongruent elements. The incongruity, in other words, is not an end in itself, but a means to an end. It is AGGRESSIVE. 2) The satirist is more relentless than the comic writer. The object of the satire is less appeased, his crimes are less extenuated, he is not allowed to "get off the hook" as easily. The satirist returns again and again to certain themes, often repeating them in various guises, and the very doggedness of the repetition suggests that fault is being found. 3) Satire is more general in its intention than comedy. Characterization is "flatter", and a character seldom develops or evolves. *The Pickwick Papers, Joseph Andrews*, and *Don Quixote* all begin as satires, but as their authors become more and more interested in their characters as human beings, rather than types, all three books move from satire into comedy. A character in a satire may have some individualizing traits, but they are a means to an end, rather than an end in themselves. The satirist is more interested in the human frailties his characters represent than in his characters as human beings.[8]

These criteria suggest that the borderline cases I mentioned above might be classified as follows. *Decline and Fall* and *Vile Bodies* are satiric rather than comic novels because their characterization is primarily "flat", and because Waugh continually emphasizes how his modern characters not only fail to live up to the honorable standards of the past, but do not even give these standards lip-service. The reader is amused, to be sure, but he blames as well. The pieces by Swift and Pope are alike in this respect: each adopts a pattern normally used for a non-satiric work – the religious meditation and the sermon, respectively – and fills it with trivial matter. In either case one might argue that there is an object of the satire, but the main emphasis seems to be upon incongruity for its own sake. Both works seem to stand outside the boundaries of satire proper. Both Falstaff and the Wife of Bath are presented in ways that suggest a satiric intention, but both are too triumphantly "round' to satisfactorily stand for anything but themselves, nor do Chaucer and Shakespeare seem to be presenting them with an aggressive

---

[8]   The names of characters in satire may of course form one of the tactics. Since they are often outrageously improbable, or type-labels, they help establish the "flatness" of the character. They may also be used to initiate or further any of the tactics mentioned in Chapters II through V. For example, the typical "pastoral" names which Swift gives some of the characters in his grimly sordid poems about London are themselves a device for insinuating a comment about idealized views of the human animal, and Chaucer's "Madame Eglentyne", a name common in romantic poetry, helps to suggest the mundane as distinct from the spiritual qualities in the nun's character.

intention. Both belong to comedy rather than satire.

So far I have been discussing the relationship of indirect satire with various other literary perspectives. Let me conclude by mentioning a suggestive difference between satire and what is not, strictly speaking, a "literary" perspective at all – what might be called "unintentional satire". Satire employs various tactics to make a deviation from a norm seem blameworthy. Sometimes a natural deviation occurs which so contrasts with what we feel is normal or "right" that the incident might well be part of an indirect satire.

Dr. Arbuthnot wrote Swift in 1714 about a scheme proposed by William Whiston and Humphrey Ditton, two well-known scientists. They had proposed, in all seriousness, a plan which would enable mariners to determine their longitude. Ships were to be anchored at each degree of the meridian and would fire rockets and discharge cannon each day at noon. Sailors in the vicinity would be able to get a "fix" from the anchored ships and thus determine their own relative positions. Arbuthnot complained that the Whiston-Ditton scheme was so absurd that it spoiled one of his Scriblerian papers.[9] A modern satirist might echo Dr. Arbuthnot's complaint. Perfectly straightforward accounts of the use to which American foreign aid is put in some of the countries of Southeast Asia and of the methods of political campaigning in some African or South American countries, or the American Deep South, make these things seem absurd to the point of farce. Accounts like these can be adapted for the purpose of satire and, indeed, frequently are. But are they satire as they stand?

What Roger Fry has to say about similar phenomena in the visual arts is relevant here. In *Vision and Design* he meets the objection that the qualities he finds in a "work of art" also occur spontaneously in the natural world – in flowers, for instance. "But in our reaction to a work of art there is something more – there is the consciousness of purpose, the consciousness of a peculiar relation of sympathy with the man who made this thing in order to arouse precisely the sensations we experience."[10]

The awareness of "consciousness of purpose" is essential in indirect satire as well. The reader becomes conscious not only of a deviation from a norm, but of a deviation consciously manipulated to produce the

---

[9] Arbuthnot's letter is quoted on p. 343 of *Memoirs of the Extraordinary Life, Works, and Discoveries of Martinus Scriblerus*, ed. Charles Kerby-Miller (New Haven, 1950). Kerby-Miller discusses the Whiston-Ditton project on pp. 334-335.
[10] "An Essay in Aesthetics", in *Vision and Design* (New York, n.d.), p. 30.

satiric effect. Part of his pleasure arises from his awareness that the manipulation is taking place – that satiric tactics are being used. The manipulator of the tactics – the writer – has created the thing to which he responds and thus it is not perverse to say that the writer of the satire and the reader must have "a peculiar relation of sympathy" in indirect satire, even though the effect of this relationship is to reduce or kill sympathy for the object of the satire.

The contrast with direct satire is marked. Except in the rare cases in which the reader recognizes himself as the object of the satire (and, as Swift remarked, "Satyr is a sort of Glass, wherein Beholders do generally discover every body's Face but their Own . . .".[11]), the reader stands outside the action. He has a ringside seat, to be sure, watching the satirist at work and enjoying the fireworks, but does not participate actively in the action itself.

In indirect satire the reader IS involved. The tactics the satirist uses create a sort of spark-gap beween insinuation and understanding. Though the gap is set up for his benefit, the reader must bridge it himself, and to do this must cooperate with the satirist; he must assume, at least for the time being, the satirist's perspective as his own. The reader's cooperation is essential; without it, the satire will not work properly. Thus he participates actively, becoming in a very real sense an aggressor himself. This involvement and participation in the satire creates an intensity of effect which is the real hallmark of successful satire.

[11] Preface to *The Battle of the Books, Prose Works*, I (1957), 140.

BIBLIOGRAPHY

Arrowsmith, William, "Introduction" to *The Satyricon* of Petronius (New York: New American Library, 1960).

Aubin, Robert A., "A Note on the Eighteenth Century Progress Pieces", *Modern Language Notes*, XLIX (1934), 405-407.

Auden, W. H., *The Dyer's Hand and Other Essays* (New York: Random House, 1962).

Austen, Jane, *The Complete Novels of Jane Austen* (New York: Modern Library, n.d.).

Beaumont, Charles Allen, *Swift's Classical Rhetoric*, University of Georgia Monographs, No. 8 (Athens, Georgia: University of Georgia Press, 1961).

Bergson, Henri, *Laughter*, in *Comedy*, Introduction and Appendix by Wylie Sypher (Garden City, New York: Doubleday and Company, 1956).

Bond, Richmond P., *English Burlesque Poetry, 1700-1750*, Harvard Studies in English, Vol. VI (Cambridge: Harvard University Press, 1932).

Booth, Wayne C., *The Rhetoric of Fiction* (Chicago: University of Chicago Press, 1961).

Brevold, Louis I., "A Note in Defense of Satire", *ELH, A Journal of English Literary History*, VII (1940), 253-264.

Brown, Wallace Cable, *Charles Churchill: Poet, Rake, and Rebel* (Lawrence: University of Kansas Press, 1953).

Burns, Robert, *The Poems of Robert Burns and Selected Letters*, ed. Anthony Hepburn (London and Glasgow: Collins, 1959).

Butler, Samuel, *Characters and Passages from Note-Books*, ed. A. R. Waller (Cambridge: Cambridge University Press, 1908).

——, *Hudibras*, notes and a literary memoir by Rev. Treadway Russel Nash, D.D. (New York: D. Appleton, 1864).

——, *Satires and Miscellaneous Poetry and Prose*, ed. René Lamar (Cambridge: Cambridge University Press, 1928).

Butler, Samuel, *Erewhon and Erewhon Revisited* (New York: Modern Library, 1927).

Byron, Lord, *Don Juan and Other Satirical Poems*, ed. Louis I. Bredvold (New York: The Odyssey Press, 1935).

Cazamian, Louis F., *The Development of English Humor* (Durham: Duke University Press, 1952).

Chaucer, Geoffrey, *The Poetical Works of Chaucer*, ed. F. N. Robinson (Cambridge, Mass.: Riverside Press, 1933).

Chesterton, G. K., "Pope and the Art of Satire", *Varied Types* (New York: Dodd, Mead & Co., 1905).

Churchill, Charles, *The Poetical Works of Charles Churchill*, ed. Douglas Grant (Oxford: Clarendon Press, 1956).

Clark, Donald Leman, *Rhetoric in Greco-Roman Education* (New York: Columbia University Press, 1957).

Crawford, Thomas, *Burns: A Study of the Poems and Songs* (Edinburgh: Oliver and Boyd, 1960).

Daiches, David, *Robert Burns* (New York: Rinehart, 1950).

Davis, Herbert, *Jonathan Swift: Essays on His Satire and Other Studies* (New York: Oxford University Press, 1964).

DeArmond, Anna Janney, "Some Aspects of Character-Writing in the Period of the Restoration", *Delaware Notes*, 16th Series (Newark: University of Delaware, 1943).

Defoe, Daniel, *The Shortest Way with the Dissenters and Other Pamphlets, The Novels and Selected Writings of Daniel Defoe*, Vol. XIV (Oxford: Basil Blackwell, 1927).

Donaldson, E. Talbot, "Chaucer the Pilgrim", *PMLA*, LXIX (1954), 928-36.

Dryden, John, "A Discourse Concerning the Original and Progress of Satire", *Essays of John Dryden*, Vol. II, ed. W. P. Ker (Oxford: Clarendon Press, 1900).

——, *The Poetical Works of Dryden*, ed. George R. Noyes (Cambridge: Riverside Press, 1950).

Edrich, Emanuel, "George Orwell and the Satire in Horror", *Texas Studies in Literature and Language*, IV (1962), 96-108.

Elliott, Robert C., *The Power of Satire: Magic, Ritual, Art* (Princeton: Princeton University Press, 1960).

Ewald, William Bragg, Jr., *The Masks of Jonathan Swift* (Cambridge: Harvard University Press, 1954).

Feinberg, Leonard, *The Satirist* (Ames, Iowa: Iowa State University Press, 1963).

Fielding, Henry, *The Adventures of Joseph Andrews*, World's Classics No. 334 (Oxford: Oxford University Press, 1929).

Freedman, Lila Hermann, *Satiric Personae: A Study in Point of View in Formal Verse Satire in the English Renaissance from Wyatt to Marston* (Ph.D. diss., University of Wisconsin, 1955).

Freud, Sigmund, *Jokes and Their Relation to the Unconscious*, trans. and ed. James Strachey (New York: W. W. Norton and Company, 1963).

Fry, Roger, "An Essay in Aesthetics", *Vision and Design* (New York: Brentano's, n.d.).

Frye, Northrop, *The Anatomy of Criticism* (Princeton: Princeton University Press, 1957).

Fuess, Claude M., *Lord Byron as a Satirist in Verse* (New York: Columbia University Press, 1912).

Gibson, Dan, Jr., "Samuel Butler", *Seventeenth Century Studies*, ed. Robert Shafer (Princeton: Princeton University Press for the University of Cincinnati, 1933).

Goldsmith, Oliver, *Goldsmith: Selected Works*, ed. Richard Garnett (London: R. Hart-Davis, 1950).

Goodman, Paul, *The Structure of Literature* (Chicago: University of Chicago Press, 1954).

Griffith, Reginald Harvey, "The Progress Pieces of the Eighteenth Century", *The Texas Review*, V (1920), 218-233.

Heiserman, A. R., *Skelton and Satire* (Chicago: University of Chicago Press, 1961).

Henry, O., *The Four Million* (New York: A. L. Burt, 1906).

Highet, Gilbert, *The Anatomy of Satire* (Princeton: Princeton University Press, 1962).

Hoffman, Arthur W., "Chaucer's Prologue to Pilgrimage: The Two Voices", *ELH, A Journal of English Literary History*, XXI (1954), 1-16.

Holloway, John, "The Well-Filled Dish: An Analysis of Swift's Satire", *Hudson Review*, IX (1956), 20-37.

Huxley, Aldous, *Brave New World* (New York and London: Harper & Brothers, 1932).

Jack, Ian, *Augustan Satire: Intention and Idiom in English Poetry, 1660-1750* (Oxford: Clarendon Press, 1952).

Johnson, Maurice, *The Sin of Wit: Jonathan Swift as a Poet* (Syracuse: Syracuse University Press, 1950).

Johnson, Samuel, *Rasselas, Poems, and Selected Prose*, ed. Bertrand H. Bronson (New York and Toronto: Rinehart, 1959).

Kernan, Alvin, *The Cankered Muse: Satire of the English Renaissance*, Yale Studies in English, Vol. # 142 (New Haven: Yale University Press, 1959).

Knox, E. V., *The Mechanism of Satire* (Cambridge: Cambridge University Press, 1951).

Landa, Louis A., "*A Modest Proposal* and Populousness", *Modern Philology*, XL (1942), 161-170.

Lawlor, John, "Radical Satire and the Realistic Novel", *Essays and Studies, New Series*, VIII (1955), 58-75.

Leavis, F. R., *Revaluation: Tradition and Development in English Poetry* (London: Chatto and Windus, 1959).

Lewis, Wyndham, *Rude Assignment: A Narrative of My Career Up-to-Date* (London: Hutchinson and Company, n.d.).

Leyburn, Ellen Douglass, *Satiric Allegory: Mirror of Man*, Yale Studies in English, Vol. 130 (New Haven: Yale University Press, 1956).

Mack Maynard, "The Muse of Satire", *Yale Review*, XLI (1951), 80-92.

——, " 'Wit and Poetry and Pope': Some Observations on His Imagery", *Eighteenth Century English Literature: Modern Essays in Criticism*, ed. James L. Clifford (New York: Oxford University Press, 1959).

Major, John M., "The Personality of Chaucer the Pilgrim", *PMLA*, LXXV (1960), 160-162.

Meredith, George, *An Essay on Comedy*, in *Comedy*, Introduction and Appendix by Wylie Sypher (Garden City, New York: Doubleday and Company, 1956).

Monk, Samuel Holt, "The Pride of Lemuel Gulliver", *Sewanee Review*, LXIII (1955), 48-71.

Muscatine, Charles, *Chaucer and the French Tradition: A Study in Style and Meaning* (Berkeley and Los Angeles: University of California Press, 1957).

Olson, Elder, "Rhetoric and the Appreciation of Pope", *Modern Philology*, XXXVII (1939), 13-35.

Paulson, Ronald, Review of *Swift and the Satirist's Art* by Edward W. Rosenheim, Jr., *Journal of English and Germanic Philology*, LXIII, No. 1 (1964), 169-176.

Peake, Charles, "Swift and the Passions", *Modern Language Review*, LV (1960), 169-180.

Peter, John D., *Complaint and Satire in Early English Literature* (Oxford: Clarendon Press, 1956).

Pope, Alexander, *The Art of Sinking in Poetry: Martinus Scriblerus' Peri Bathous*, ed. Edna Leake Steeves (New York: Columbia University Press, 1952).

——, *The Poems of Alexander Pope*, The Twickenham Edition, eds. John Butt *et al.*, 6 vols. (London: Methuen; New Haven: Yale University Press, 1939-61).

——, *The Prose Works of Alexander Pope*, ed. Norman Ault, Vol. I: *The Earlier Works, 1711-1720* (only Vol. I published) (Oxford: Basil Blackwell, 1936).

Potts, L. J., *Comedy* (London: Hutchinson University Library, 1949).

Price, Martin, *Swift's Rhetorical Art: A Study in Structure and Meaning*, Yale

Studies in English, Vol. 123 (New Haven: Yale University Press, 1953).

Quintana, Ricardo, *The Mind and Art of Jonathan Swift* (New York: Oxford University Press, 1936).

——, "Samuel Butler: A Restoration Figure in a Modern Light", *ELH, A Journal of English Literary History*, XVIII (1951), 7-31.

——, "Situational Satire: A Commentary on the Method of Swift", *University of Toronto Quarterly*, XVII (1948), 130-136.

——, *Swift: An Introduction* (London: Oxford University Press, 1955).

Randolph, Mary Claire, " 'Candour' in XVIIIth-century Satire", *Review of English Studies*, XX (1944), 45-62.

——, "The Sinful Suburbs of Cookery: Satirical Recipes of the XVIIIth Century", *Notes and Queries*, CLXXXVI (1944), 32-36.

——, "The Structural Design of the Formal Verse Satire", *Philological Quarterly*, XXI (1942), 368-384.

Richards, Edward Ames, *Hudibras in the Burlesque Tradition*, Columbia University Studies in English and Comparative Literature, Vol. 127 (New York: Columbia University Press, 1937).

Rosenheim, Edward W. Jr., *Swift and the Satirist's Art* (Chicago: University of Chicago Press, 1963).

Sacheverell, Henry, *The Political Union* (London: 1710).

Sams, Henry W., "Swift's Satire of the Second Person", *ELH, A Journal of English Literary History*, XXVI (1959), 36-44.

Scriblerus Club, Members of the, *Memoirs of the Extraordinary Life, Works, and Discoveries of Martinus Scriblerus*, ed. Charles Kerby-Miller (New Haven: Yale University Press for Wellesley College, 1950).

Sedgwick, G. G., *Of Irony, Especially in Drama*, University of Toronto Studies, No. 10 (Toronto: University of Toronto Press, 1935).

Sharpe, Robert Boies, *Irony in the Drama: An Essay on Impersonation, Shock and Catharsis* (Chapel Hill: University of North Carolina Press, 1959).

Sherburn, George, *The Early Career of Alexander Pope* (Oxford: Clarendon Press, 1934).

Slepian, Barry, "The Ironic Intention of Swift's Verses on His Own Death", *Review of English Studies*, N.S., XIV, No. 55 (1963), 249-256.

Stamm, Rudolph G., "Daniel Defoe: An Artist in the Puritan Tradition", *Philological Quarterly*, XV (1936), 225-246.

Starkman, Miriam Kosh, *Swift's Satire on Learning in A Tale of a Tub* (Princeton: Princeton University Press, 1950).

Stopp, Frederick J., *Evelyn Waugh: Portrait of an Artist* (London: Chapman and Hall, 1958).

Sutherland, James, *Defoe* (Philadelphia and New York: J. B. Lippincott, 1938).

——, *English Satire* (Cambridge: Cambridge University Press, 1958).

Swayne, Mattie, "The Progress Piece in the Seventeenth Century", *University of Texas Bulletin: Studies in English*, No. 16 (1936), 84-92.

Swift, Jonathan, *Gulliver's Travels: The Text of the First Edition*, ed. Harold Williams (London: First Edition Club, 1926).

——, *The Poems of Jonathan Swift*, 2nd ed., ed. Harold Williams, 3 vols. (Oxford: Clarendon Press, 1958).

——, *The Prose Works of Jonathan Swift*, ed. Herbert Davis, 13 vols. (Oxford: Basil Blackwell, 1939-62).

——, *Satires and Personal Writings*, ed. William Alfred Eddy (London and New York: Oxford University Press, 1937).

Thompson, Alan Reynolds, *The Dry Mock: A Study of Irony in Drama* (Berkeley and Los Angeles: University of California Press, 1948).

Thomson, J. A. K., *Irony: An Historical Introduction* (London: G. Allen & Unwin, 1926).

Tindall, William York, *A Reader's Guide to James Joyce* (New York: Noonday Press, 1959).

Waith, Eugene M., *The Pattern of Tragicomedy in Beaumont and Fletcher*, Yale Studies in English, Vol. 120 (New Haven: Yale University Press, 1952).

Walker, Hugh, *English Satire and Satirists* (London and Toronto: J. M. Dent & Sons; New York: E. P. Dutton, 1925).

Warren, Austin, "Alexander Pope", *Rage for Order: Essays in Criticism* (Chicago: University of Chicago Press, 1948).

Waugh, Evelyn, *Decline and Fall* (Harmondsworth, Middlesex: Penguin Books, 1951).

——, *The Loved One: An Anglo-American Tragedy* (Harmondsworth, Middlesex: Penguin Books, 1951).

——, *Vile Bodies* (Harmondsworth, Middlesex: Penguin Books, 1938).

Wellek, René, and Austin Warren, *Theory of Literature* (New York: Harcourt, Brace and Company, 1956).

Winters, Yvor, "The Poetry of Charles Churchill", *Poetry*, Vol. 98, No. 1 (April, 1961), 44-53; and Vol. 98, No. 2 (May, 1961), 104-117.

Wolfe, Humbert, *Notes on English Verse Satire* (New York: Harcourt, Brace and Company, 1929).

Worcester, David, *The Art of Satire* (New York: Russell and Russell, 1960).

Wordsworth, William, *The Poetical Works of Wordsworth*, ed. Thomas Hutchinson (New York: Oxford, 1933).

Yunck, John A., "The Two Faces of Parody", *Iowa English Yearbook, No. 8* (Fall, 1963), 29-37.

INDEX

DE PROPRIETATIBUS LITTERARUM

edited by

C. H. VAN SCHOONEVELD

Series Maior

1. Marcus B. Hester, *The Meaning of Poetic Metaphor: An Analysis in the Light of Wittgenstein's Claim that Meaning is Use.* 1967. 229 pp.
   f 36.— / $ 10.00

2. Rodney Delasanta, *The Epic Voice.* 1967. 140 pp.   *f* 22.— / $ 5.75

3. Bennison Gray, *Style: The Problem and its Solution.* 1969. 117 pp.
   f 23.— / $ 6.50

5. Raimund Belgardt, *Romantische Poesie: Begriff und Bedeutung bei Friedrich Schlegel.* 1970. 257 pp.   *f* 45.— / $ 12.50

Series Minor

1. Trevor Eaton, *The Semantics of Literature.* 1966. 72 pp.
   f 10.— / $ 2.80

2. Walter A. Koch, *Recurrence and a Three-Modal Approach to Poetry.* 1966. 57 pp.   *f* 10.— / $ 2.80

3. Nancy Sullivan, *Perspective and the Poetic Process.* 1968. 56 pp.
   f 10.— / $ 2.80

4. Donald LoCicero, *Novellentheorie: The Practicality of the Theoretical.* 1970. 120 pp.   *f* 16.— / $ 4.50

Series Practica

1. Robert G. Cohn, *Mallarmé's Masterpiece: New Findings.* 1966. 114 pp.
   f 22.— / $ 5.75

2. Constance B. Hieatt, *The Realism of Dream Vision: The Poetic Exploitation of the Dream-Experience in Chaucer and His Contemporaries.* 1967. 112 pp.   *f* 16.— / $ 4.50

3. Joseph J. Mogan Jr., *Chaucer and the Theme of Mutability*. 1969. 190 pp.   f 26.— / $ 7.45

4. Peter Nusser, *Musils Romantheorie*. 1967. 114 pp.   f 18.— / $ 5.00

5. Marjorie Perloff, *Rhyme and Meaning in the Poetry of Yeats*. 1970. 249 pp.   f 48.— / $ 13.75

6. Marian H. Cusac, *Narrative Structure in the Novels of Sir Walter Scott*. 1969. 128 pp.   f 20.— / $ 5.75

8. W. Victor Wortley, *Tallement des Réaux: The Man through his Style*. 1969. 99 pp.   f 22.— / $ 6.30

9. Donald R. Swanson, *Three Conquerors: Character and Method in the Mature Works of George Meredith*. 1969. 148 pp.   f 22.— / $ 6.30

10. Irwin Gopnik, *A Theory of Style and Richardson's Clarissa*. 1970. 140 pp.   f 22.— / $ 6.30

12. Sylvia D. Feldman, *The Morality-Patterned Comedy of the Renaissance*. 1971. 165 pp.   f 18.— / $ 5.00

13. Giles Mitchell, *The Art Theme in Joyce Cary's First Trilogy*. 1971. 136 pp.   f 18.— / $ 5.00

17. Meredith B. Raymond, *Swinburne's Poetics: Theory and Practice*. 1971. 202 pp.   f 36.—

20. Edgar B. Schick, *Metaphorical Organicism in Herder's Early Works: A Study of the Relation of Herder's Literary Idiom to His World-view*. 1971. 135 pp.   f 25.— / $ 6.95

22. James E. Magner Jr., *John Crowe Ransom: Critical Principles and Pre-occupations*. 1971. 134 pp.   f 18.— / $ 5.00

23. Elisabeth Th. M. van de Laar, *The Inner Structure of Wuthering Heights: A Study of an Imaginative Field*. 1969. 262 pp.   f 36.— / $ 10.00

24. Bernard L. Einbond, *Samuel Johnson's Allegory*. 1971. 104 pp.   f 18.— / $ 5.00

27. Richard Vernier, *'Poésie ininterrompue' et la poétique de Paul Eluard*. 1971. 180 pp.   f 25.— / $ 6.95

28. Hugh L. Hennedy, *Unity in Barsetshire*. 1971. 144 pp. f 28.— / $ 7.90

35. Roman Jakobson and Lawrence G. Jones, *Shakespeare's Verbal Art in Th'Expence of Spirit*. 1970. 32 pp.   f 10.— / $ 2.90

MOUTON · PUBLISHERS · THE HAGUE